UNDER THE PARISH LANTERN

Llanilltud Faerdref Parish in Pictures

by

DILLWYN LEWIS

1981

DILLWYN LEWIS
12 LLANTRISANT ROAD
BEDDAU, PONTYPRIDD
MID. GLAMORGAN CF38 2BB

ISBN 0 9500567 2 3

Printed in Great Britain by
The Starling Press Ltd, Risca, Newport, Gwent NP1 6YB

For My Dear Grandparents
Evan and Priscilla Roberts
and
Richard and Hannah Lewis
and
All Parishioners
Past, Present and Future
who work for the well-being
of the Parish.

Acknowledgements

The Author acknowledges the assistance of Sir Cennydd Traherne, K.G., T.D., Lord Lieutenant of the Counties of Glamorgan; Rt. Hon. Brynmor John, M.P. for Pontypridd Constituency; Rev. A. J. D. Williams, B.A., Vicar of Llanilltud Faerdref; The Glamorgan Archive Service; Victoria & Albert Museum, London; National Library, Aberystwyth; Powell Duffryn Ltd.; Celtic Press Ltd.; Western Mail & Echo Ltd.; H. Tempest Ltd.; Mid Glamorgan County Council; Taff Ely Borough Council; Llanilltud Faerdref Community Council; Church Village W.I.; Mrs. Dilys Webb for Cwm Rhondda material and permission to use facsimile of original manuscript; Mrs. E. Clapp for Cwm Colliery material; John Fortt, Esq. for sketch of Ida House; Mr. Cyril Bernard and The Teacher magazine; Alvis Edwards, Esq.; John S. George, Esq.; Derek Lewis, Esq.; William John Lewis, Esq., J.P.; Miss Eileen Perkins; Miss Margaret Jenkins, Wellfield; John Collins, Esq., Tynant; Martyn Astrand, Esq.; Trevor Absolom, Esq.; George Lane, Esq.; Idris Evans, Esq.

The Author wishes to record his very special thanks to Mr. William Richards, A.R.P.S., Mr. Howard Withers and Mr. Cecil Williams for their technical skill in preparing photographs for this book. Furthermore, the Author wishes to express his most grateful thanks and appreciation for the encouragement of everyone and to all those who so generously tendered information and submitted photographs for inclusion in this book.

Poems included by permission of William John Lewis, J.P. (Gwilym Llaeron). Mr. Lewis is descended from Ieuan Gwyllt (John Roberts) who inaugurated Cymanfa Ganu and is well known as a Welsh hymn-writer. My best thanks to Mrs. Pat Baxter for typing the script. Acknowledgement is made of the work of E. Hayward, T. Forrest, Ernest T. Bush and F. Frith &

Co. whose views were popular during various periods. I wish to express my personal thanks to colleagues in schools in the Parish for loaning examples from school archives.

D.L.

Foreword

SIR CENNYDD TRAHERNE, K.G., T.D.

Her Majesty's Lord-Lieutenant for
The Counties of Glamorgan.

I have much pleasure in acceding to Mr. Dillwyn Lewis's request to write a short Foreword to his "History of Llantwit Fardre".

This excellent History will be a companion volume to the Author's "History of Beddau and District" and "History of Llantrisant and District" published in 1965 and 1966 respectively and also to the new and revised edition of "A History of Llantrisant" published in 1975.

This new "History of Llantwit Fardre" will record many matters of historical and local interest which might otherwise be lost to future generations of inhabitants of this place.

Famous men have lived in Llantwit Fardre, including Mr. Powell, one of the Founders of the famous Powell Duffryn Company, affectionately known in former years as the "P.D.", the largest Mine-owning concern in South Wales and another famous name comes to my mind, that of John Hughes the Composer of "Cwm Rhondda" which is sung in Church and Chapel and at all places where Welshmen meet together, like before the internationals at Cardiff Arms Park.

I would like to congratulate the Author on having collected so many interesting photographs which give considerable interest to his work.

I wish its publication every success.

Publisher's Note

Reproduction of some of these photographs has been impaired due to age. They are included however since it is important to have them as historical records. The reader is requested to make allowances when bearing this in mind, since the Printers have attempted to overcome this difficulty. Blurred images and variations in tone are due to faulty photographs and are not the product of printing inadequacies.

Contents

Preface

Rt. Hon. Brynmor John, M.P.
Member for the Pontypridd Constituency

Local history has the fascination of the unexpected. We are, all through our schooldays, aware of some of the great events which have world shattering impacts. Our capacity for being surprised at facts about the area in which we live, and therefore, should know best, is great and surprising—especially to ourselves.

This will, I prophesy be the effect on those who read this book. Even the oldest inhabitant will find something he or she did not know and for the many newcomers to this Parish it will give a sense of history and continuity to their residence.

We are doubly fortunate now. For many hundreds of years the idea that men had of their ancestors and the world in which they lived depended upon the word pictures of historians (often subjective) and the painted pictures of men and places (often idealized). For the last hundred years or so the photograph has enabled us to get an accurate observation of the past. Hence the endless fascination of old photographs for people, the world has changed more rapidly in the last century than in all its previous history and often incomprehension of the recent past would otherwise be profound.

Combine the two elements together, as Dillwyn Lewis has in this book, and you get a portrait of a parish, part rural, part industrial, part quiet village, part bustling manufacture, which gives a vivid picture of the last century—the cauldron of change.

It is now captured in this book, and in a way that future generations will appreciate.

Dillwyn Lewis, already one of the most distinguished local historians, has added to his reputation and placed us further in his debt for this splendid book.

Introduction

Rev. A. J. D. Williams, B.A.
Vicar of the Parish of
Llanilltud Faerdref.
Freeman of Llantrisant.

It is a great privilege and joy to have been asked to write an introductory note for this important book which sets out to depict photographically some of the history of this ancient parish of Llanilltud Faerdref. This attempt to set down the history of the area in such a way, is obviously limited because it depends on past and present photographs, photography itself spanning only a hundred and fifty years.

The author, Mr. Dillwyn Lewis, a local historian of repute, is very conscious of this and is at present writing a detailed history of our area. This will enable us to realise that Llanilltud Faerdref community was in existence long before the Norman conquest, and was a community of no mean influence.

It is important that present inhabitants of Llanilltud Faerdref should know the value of the heritage which they enjoy. They should be aware of the forces and influences which moulded the past, resulting in our present society. The author is to be congratulated on his wisdom in searching carefully over the past few years to bring together yesterday's mementos. The inhabitants, some who have since died, have been most generous and practical with their helpful co-operation in loaning their photographs. The book gives an impression of a well-ordered society by whose labours our present day has been greatly enhanced. The changing life of the community is portrayed over the years, the growth of industry, the cultural heritage, the religious, educational, and commercial progress. We are reminded of certain gifted individuals who in their different ways have influenced their community. We are shown fleeting glimpses of the past but within this book we see life in a community in all its manifold variety and richness. It points us to the past bidding us to be grateful for, and proud of our heritage, and then look with faith and courage to the future.

It is a book for the young with the hope that it will arouse in them a keen interest in the influences, events and movements out of which Llanilltud Faerdref evolved. Also to awaken in them a sense of pride in the best traditions of the past with a deep concern for the future. Its publication has been awaited by the older members of our community with great anticipation, and they, too, can look through the pages with gratitude and pride in the richness of a community of which they, as individuals, have played their part.

The Llanilltud Faerdref Community Council are to be congratulated for graciously sponsoring the book and the author, in his generosity, deciding to donate the proceeds from the book, towards the Restoration Fund of the Parish Church. It is published to mark the major restoration and extension of the oldest building in the Parish—the Parish Church of St. Illtud—which down through the generations, has played such a prominent role in the life of the Community.

The Churchwardens, Parochial Church Councillors and I are grateful to Mr. Dillwyn Lewis and to the Community Council for their magnificent gesture. To Mr. Dillwyn Lewis a special thank you for a book of immense historical importance in recording for all time the life of our Community.

"There is no past, so long as books shall live."

Lynton—The Soul of Books.

Dillwyn Lewis preparing photographs of History of Llantwit Fardre Parish

The Parish of Llanilltud-y-Faerdref

The Parish of Llanilltud-y-Faerdref has been remarkable for its beautiful rural scenery while underground were sources of prosperity waiting discovery and speculation. The first farmers began to arrive in South Wales about 3000 B.C. Their most impressive remains were cromlechs, one of which can be seen at Caeryrfa, Creigiau. Cairns are to be seen on Garth Mountain. In a cave here, a small, knobbed pot of Late Bronze Age type has been found. Several earthworks can be seen, especially, the Iron Age hillforts at Castellau and Caerau east of Llantrisant. Evidence of Roman occupation has also been discovered.

Although Christianity was introduced before the Romans left, credit for converting the Welsh must go to the Celtic saints, who, in the fifth and sixth centuries worked to establish centres in the hill country. One of these centres was Llanilltud Faerdref.

The Parish Church is dedicated to St. Illtyd, celebrated as the Saint of the Five Keys of Youth, Learning, Chivalry, Priesthood, and Knighthood, whose memory is associated with the fifth-century monastic college at Llantwit Major. The church is on a site that has been used for worship since the fifth century although the present building dates only from 1525. The oldest part is the nave with a rather fine barrel-vaulted roof of perfect semi-circular proportions. The tower dates from 1636; the registers from 1632, whilst the 16th century chalice and paten are still in use. The church is said to be one of the finest examples of Laudian architecture in Wales. It has recently been restored and rededicated in 1974. A sister church, dedicated to St. Andrew, was opened in 1914 at Newtown, Llantwit. Throughout the district names remind us that the surrounding places were subjected to attacks and ancient battle sites are marked. In A.D. 721, a battle was fought on Garth Maelwg and in A.D. 873 the Battle of Rhiwsaeson (Saxons' Slope) was fought.

After the end of the Roman occupation about 410 A.D., a line of Welsh kings of the 'gwlad' of Glamorgan developed. The Welsh kingdom continued until 1090, when the Norman lord, Robert Fitzhamon, Earl of Gloucester invaded Glamorgan. The Vale of Glamorgan was divided between some of Robert Fitzhamon's followers, but the hill country remained in the hands of the local Welsh rulers. By the thirteenth century, however, the lord was ordered to subdue and control even the hill country and castles at Llantrisant and Caerphilly were established as symbols of authority in this district. During this period, land was divided into Commotes and Cantrefs (Hundreds) which was the Welsh custom:—

10 houses	—	1 tref (town)
10 trefs	—	1 commote
10 commotes	—	1 cantref
10 cantrefs	—	1 gwlad, cyfoeth, arglwydd (lordship)

Llantwit Fardre was situated in the Trissent Hundred in the Lordship of Glamorgan. This land system was established by Hywel Dda's Venedotian Code about the year 940.

Wales was divided into 52 territorial divisions (cantrefs or hundreds) which consisted of two *Cymwds* or Commotes—these were sub-divided into *Maenols*.

Laws of Measure:

4 acres to every tyddyn (Tenement)
16 acres to every randir (Shareland)
64 acres to every gavael (holding)
256 acres to every trev (township)
4 trevs (1,024 acres) to each Maenol
1 Cymwd contained 12 Maenols and 2 trevs (12,800 acres).

Of the 12 Maenols which were in the cymwd, 4 were assigned to aillts (villeins) to support dogs and horses, and for dovraeth (quarters); and one for Canghellorship and one for Maership and the rest for free Uchelwrs (freemen). The two trevs are for use of the king; one of them to be maentrev land for him and the other to be the King's waste (diffaith brenin) and summer pasture (havodtir).

Maentrev was that portion of each cymwd surrendered to the king or prince and forming his estate or demesne. Llanilltyd Faerdref is the Church of St. Illtyd situated within the township or demesne of the king or prince.

There were two 'Maers' in connection with the king's domains—Maer and Maer biswail (bailiff of the cow-lair)—an officer attached to the court received the cattle purveyed for the lords and superintended the demesne lands.

The Maer who resided in the Maertrev was accompanied by another officer called a Canghellor who "held pleas to determine disputes among the king's villeins and secured his wastes".

These two offices were filled by "uchelwrs" (freemen) and not by chiefs of a kindred. They were to superintend their district and form the courts. Everything received by the king was to be divided—half to the king and half to the Maer and Canghellor excepting the "Worth of land"; the "worth of a thief and the worth of a dead body". They were allowed to keep two servants to enforce their commands and two others were to be retained for the king. They were to make a progress in parties of four amongst the king's aillts twice annually. They received half the ebediw (heriot) of the aillts and half the amobyr (marriage fee) of their daughters. At the death of an aillt, the Maer and Canghellor divided his land according to the law. They were to keep the king's waste and swear for him when necessary.

Maer-biswail or land maer was chosen from among the aillts. He superintended the court under the dystain (steward) and received things brought to him by the maer and canghellor for the court. He regulated ploughing, sowing, tending the king's cattle, etc. He punished the men of the maentrev for any illegalities. He was to defend the purveyance land of the Court when necessary together with summer pasture and other things which may pertain to them.

He received the whole cambwrw, dirwy (fines) and ebediw of the maentrev and his wife the amobyr of their daughters, while the men of the maertrev were to supply him with gwestva (entertainment). He was not to hold courts except upon the men of the Maertrev.

The men of the Maertrev should build a drying kiln and a barn for the king and should supply them when necessary. They should pay fealty of their land to the maer biswail and should support him twice a year. They should thresh, kiln-dry, reap, harrow, mow the hay and each time the king came to his court they should supply straw and fuel for his use. They should present the king when he came to his court, according to their ability with sheep, lambs, kids, cheese, butter, milk.

The men of the Maentrev were not compelled to work on the castles. The king's waste or diffaith brenin was anything unowned and comprised the seas, wilds, downs, forests, highways and all unowned goods. It also included the unmarried women on account of his being the guardian of their honour and received in consequence the virgin fee (amobyr) on the marriage of everyone according to their respective ranks.

The village which grew around the residence of the maer became in time called the maerdref and grew into prominence as an agricultural centre.

Such was the establishment of Llanilltud-y-Faerdref which is reasonably translated to mean "The Church of Saint Illtud on the home farm of the Prince".

The name itself has always proved to be a subject of enquiry and discussion and over the years has been written in various spellings :—

Llanelldyd Vayrdre	1549
Llanyltiduandray	1576 (Saxton)
Lanyltidvandray	1610, 1627 (Speede)
Lanyltidvandray	1787 (John Sellar)
Llaneltid	1787 (J. Cary)
Lantwittvardre	1799 (Yates)
Llantwitt ffairdre	1832 (O.S.)
Llantwit Vaird	1835
Llantwit Vayrdre	1875
Llantwit Fardre	1976 }
Llanilltud Faerdref	

The Norman advance into Glamorgan was a decisive turning point in history. Like the Roman occupation, it was a military operation. The district increased in importance because Llantrisant was established as a garrison town and a castle built at this strategic point. There is a remains of a Motte and bailey castle to be seen at Tonteg. This provided a look-out over the Taff Valley.

During the early years of this century, Coed Twr or Tomen y Clawdd, which is now on the Oaklands Estate, still had a moat surrounding it. Near the Pound Farm and by Nant Ifan Ddu is Caer Odin Filwr.

One of the great travellers was Giraldus Cambrensis (1146-1223) who recorded in the twelfth century how the Welsh lived,

> "They neither inhabit towns, villages, nor castles, but lead a solitary life in the woods, on the borders of which they do not erect sumptious palaces, nor lofty stone buildings but content themselves with small huts made of the boughs of trees twisted together, constructed with little labour and expense, and sufficient to endure throughout the year."

All was not well and fighting frequently broke out between the Normans and the Welsh chieftains. Llewellyn Bren of Senghenydd continually resisted the Norman overlords and inflicted great destruction in the area. He also helped Owen Glyndwr in his fight against the English. It is known that Llewellyn Bren lived in the Taff Valley and it is supposed that he lived at Castell Coch (Red Castle). In a report on Llewellyn Bren's effects, submitted to Edward II in 1316, items regarding cattle, goats, horses, etc., belonging to him in Miskin (Llantrisant) and Glyn Rhondda were mentioned. In a play about Ifor Bach and the rebellion of 1316, a character named Meredith of Llantwit Vardre is mentioned.

As time passed by resistance decreased and the castles fell into disuse. Instead, the district was dotted with stately mansions, inhabited by county families. The district was ruled by the Lord of the Manor who, until 1246, was a Welshman but by 1348, the Lord was Hugh Despenser. With the Act of Union 1536, effective law and order was administered according to the Laws of the Realm. This brought the Great Session into Wales, Quarter Sessions and Justices of the Peace came into being to administer the law. Welsh talents were encouraged and supported. Wealthy families lost no opportunity to become Justices of the Peace, Sheriffs and Members of Parliament. For generations the government of the countryside was in their hands.

The office of High Sheriff has had representatives connected with Llantwit Fardre. In 1849, Robert Boteler of Llandough Castle and Maesmawr, Llantwit Fardre held the office of High Sheriff. In 1850, Rowland Fothergill of Treforest and Hensol Castle held the office.

Representatives are found to have held the Office of Under Sheriff. In effect, this office provided a deputy Sheriff and was discontinued after 1850. Evan Prichard, Diwedid, held the office in 1646 and a Charles Evans, Lantwit Fardre in 1678 and again in 1700. During his year of office in 1678, Charles Evans was among the twelve justices forming the grand jury at the priest-hunting trials of those clergy who were accused of "Popish Plots"

The Reformation ended Monastic establishments and the Tudor period was one of acquiring and consolidating estates. The modern pattern of landowner, small tenant farmer and landless labourer began to emerge. There are a number of large mansions in the district but only Castellau Fawr near Llantrisant continued to be the home of the original owning family, Lt. Col. J. L. R. Traherne until 1976.

In 1601, the Poor Law Act made parishes responsible for providing funds to care for the poor and infirm. The Church which was the centre of social life became integrated into the social services so that the Easter Vestry became the parliament of the parish. As the manor system broke up, the parish was adopted as a unit of Local Government.

The present Parish of Llantwit Fardre is bounded on the west by the Parish of Llantrisant, on the north and east by the Parish of Pontypridd and Treforest, on the south-east by the Parish of Caerphilly, and on the south by the Parish of Pentyrch. Its boundary, starting at the Cwm Road, Tynant, proceeds diagonally across to include the top end of Commercial Street and Windsor Gardens, then to the west of the Cwm Colliery up to join the Parish of Pontypridd boundary to the east of Pencoedcae. Continuing in an easterly direction the boundary goes across to the north of the Maendy Quarries and then down Nant-y-dall to Ynysgyfeillion to the River Taff near the southern fringe of Rhydyfelin. Turning downstream, and in mid-stream the line proceeds down past the Willowford to the outskirts of Glan-y-llyn, where it turns sharply up to the north of Gwaelod-y-Garth, across the northern and eastern approaches to the Garth Hill, and so down the Nant-y-felin Brook to a point to the south and west of Cwm Isaf, thence down through Coed Hendre-'scuthan and across to Tyn-y-coed to the Caesar's Arms. It continues in a north-westerly direction up Nant Myddlyn, across the branch railway line to Llantrisant, past Ystradbarwig Uchaf to the Cwm Road, Tynant.

Originally, the Parish was more extensive and is known to have included part of the old Urban District of Pontypridd. It is believed to have extended as far as High Street, Pontypridd, to a point at the junction of the Taff and Rhondda rivers. In 1848, Treforest, part of the Parish of Llantwit Fardre, was taken to form the new Parish of Glyntaff. Later in 1884, Pontypridd became a parish in its own right making Llantwit Fardre its present day size. When the new Local Government Act 1894 made Pontypridd a civil parish and an Urban District, the modern Parish of Llantwit Fardre was linked with the Parish of Llantrisant to form the new Llantrisant and Llantwit Fardre Rural District Council in 1895.

Changes were accelerated by the Civil War in 1642. Most of Glamorgan gentry fought for the King. Their arch-type in the Taff-Ely Borough was Judge David Jenkins of Hensol who declared himself ready to die on the scaffold for his cause with a Bible under one arm and a copy of the Magna Carta under the other! King Charles I, in 1648 on his way to the Battle of St. Fagans is reputed to have spent the night at Maesmawr Farm, Llantwit Fardre. There is a room there known as the King's Room and the land has been farmed by the same family for over 500 years.

With a Puritan Victory, the congregations of Dissenters grew apace. The Quakers found support and there are ruins of a Meeting House at Treferig, Castellau near Llantrisant. Cromwell ruled instead of the King. His real name was Williams and was related to the Williams family, Aberpergwm. Descendants of this family continue to reside in the district at Miskin Manor and Llanharan House.

After the Restoration of Charles II in 1660, a vicar of Llantrisant was ejected from his living and during the eighteenth century, the big landowners, the Windsors and Butes who had married the heiresses of the Lewises and Herberts became prominent.

The Deere Family has records from 1617 and shows that many members of this family spread over the Vale of Glamorgan from a main line established in Llantwit

Major in the sixteenth century. Reynold Deere, High Sheriff of Wenvoe (1684), was the grandfather of Reynold Deere (1732) of Penllyne Court. Major Reynold Thomas Deere was a second son of a James Thomas, Garth Fawr Estate in Llantwit Fardre. A forbearer of James Thomas was Major Robert Naughton, Aide de Camp to Charles II. The family is commemorated in the name—Deere Road—on the Crown Hill Estate.

The gulf between landowners and peasantry was increasing and attempts were made to raise the standard of morality and religion by teaching people to read and providing them with Bibles (S.P.C.K.). Rev. Griffith Jones (1683-1761) became famous for his system of Circulating Schools held in the church and farms in the parish during the period 1738-1755. This movement helped towards the religious revival when during the 1730's saw the birth of Welsh Methodism. A most fervent son, Hywel Harris (1714-73) travelled the district and spent a night at Ynysangharad House in what is now Pontypridd. Dafydd Jones Llangan became a staunch champion. John Wesley, the famous divine, travelled from the Vale of Glamorgan to Llantrisant through Penycoedcae to Pontypridd on horseback. The Nonconformists gained support and after meeting in farmhouses in the district began to build the familiar 'Noah Ark'-shaped chapel, bleak, bare, which became the symbol of Welsh worship and social life.

Bryntirion Chapel was established as a result of the Methodist Revival. The cause continues today at Bethesda Chapel, Llantwit.

In 1835, the Poor Law Act reorganised parishes into Unions centred on a Workhouse to shelter the poor, infirm, unemployed and homeless. This parish was part of the Merthyr Union but later the Pontypridd Union was formed eventually building the Graig Workhouse in 1865 within the boundary of Llantwit Fardre Parish.

Due to various methods, Vestries became unpopular in Stuart times and from 1697, Bills were introduced in

Parliament to control vestry powers and publish their accounts. A Bill was eventually passed.

At the end of the 19th century in 1894, Open Vestries were nearly extinct and were reorganised by Parliament as part of a new system of Local Government. This resulted in a method of Parish Government which with very little alteration, existed until 1st April, 1974, when the Local Government Reorganisation Act came into force.

People were taking greater interest in national and local affairs. All rate-payers were now entitled to vote and they wished to govern their own districts. Two Acts of Parliament, the Local Government Acts of 1888 and 1894 were responsible for organising efficient supervision of each district. By the 1888 Act, County and Borough Councils were established and the Act of 1894 established Urban, Rural District and Parish Councils. By these Acts, the Parish Vestry lost what remained of its authority and is now only concerned with church matters. The Llantrisant and Llantwit Fardre Rural District was originally part of the Pontypridd Union Rural Sanitary Authority, which comprised Eglwysilan, Llanfabon, Llantrisant, Llantwit Fardre, Llanwonno, Pontypridd and Rhondda.

The first elections for the Llantrisant and Llantwit Fardre Rural District Council were held on 17th December, 1894 and the first Council elected was as follows:—

Town Ward

Godfrey L. Clark, J.P., gentleman; Evan John, J.P., gentleman; Stephen Vivian, mining engineer.

Tonyrefail Ward

E. S. Richards, mining engineer; J. S. Williams, colliery manager; Wm. Evans, farmer.

Llantwit Fardre

Thos. Lewis, grocer; Daniel Bryant, postmaster; Lewis Williams, schoolmaster.

The first Chairman was Godfrey L. Clark, J.P. of Talygarn House, High Sheriff of Glamorgan.

The following names are members of the first Llantrisant Parish Council also elected on 17th December, 1894:—

Town (South Ward)

Charles Cooksley, builder; Thos. John, farmer; Philip John Dunn, gentleman; Rev. J. P. Hughes, vicar; John Morgan, builder; Evan Lewis, farmer; Wm. John, collier; Lewis Ajax, collier.

Tonyrefail (North Ward)

Isaac Owen, schoolmaster; Wm. Williams, colliery manager; Evan Thomas, gentleman; Robert Evans, collier; Thos. Thomas, check weigher; David Rowlands, collier; David Naunton Morgan, surgeon.

To form the District Council, the Parish of Llantrisant as it was in 1894 and the Parish of Llantwit Fardre were amalgamated:—

Llantrisant	:	14,109 acres
Llantwit Fardre	:	4,224 acres
Total area	:	18,433 acres

This authority was one of the largest of its kind in Britain. The number of councillors had doubled since the original election to 18 members who represented an estimated population of 27,680. The Council was responsible for providing houses, recreational facilities, lighting and similar services and the repair of by-roads, trimming of hedges etc. Laws passed by the National Government known as "statutory" laws are carried out in practice by the local authority while "mandatory" laws may be carried out at the option of the local authority. By this token each locality is governed in a democratic way, laws being observed and bye-laws passed by a representative body elected by the people.

At the first Meeting of the new Parish Council for the

Parish of Llantwit Fardre held at the Board School, Llantwit Fardre on Tuesday the first day of January 1895 at 7.0 p.m. the following members being present:—

Mr. William Chubb	Mr. John Bryant
Mr. Charles James	Mr. D. Martin Jones
Mr. Gwilym Lewis	Mr. Thomas Rees
Mr. John Rowlands	Mr. John Williams
Mr. Lewis Williams	Mr. William Williams

and also

The Rev. John Jenkins, Vicar, Chairman of the Parish Meeting and as Convener of the said meeting.

Mr. William Chubb was the first Chairman of the Parish Council.

Mr. Hopkin S. Davies the Clerk to Parish Council (Rate Collector for the Parish).

Representatives on the last Parish Council of Llantwit Fardre to meet on Tuesday 13th February 1974 in the Parish Hall, formerly the Parish Library, were:—

Councillor	— Joseph Arnold	Church Village
	— Leslie Boldero	Llantwit Fardre
	— Eric C. M. Harte	Efail Isaf
	— David Hughes, J.P.	Church Village
	— Luther Lodwig	Church Village
	— D. Brian Millward	Church Village
	— Thomas J. Rees	Church Village
	— G. Llewellyn Thomas	Church Village
	— Robert W. Thomas	Church Village
	—*Royston J. Gregory	Church Village
	— Mrs. Marilyn Watkins	Efail Isaf

* Councillor R. J. Gregory was co-opted on to the Council to fill the vacancy created by the tragic death of Councillor W. Trevor Jones, The Parade, Church Village.

The Chairman was Councillor G. L. Thomas, Church Village and the Parish Clerk, Mr. W. H. Jones.

The last officers of L.R.D.C. were:—

Clerk to the Council:	W. I. Maddocks, Esq.
Engineer & Surveyor:	T. J. Hopkins, B.Sc.
Treasurer & Accountant:	R. J. Brown, F.I.M.T.A., D.P.A.
Medical Officer of Health:	Dr. Eileen G. Watkins, M.B., B.Ch., B.A.O., D.P.H., L.M.(R.O.T.)

The Chief Officer of the new Taff-Ely Borough Council is Geoffrey Hockin, Esq., B.A. He was the former Clerk to the Llantrisant Rural District Council. The first Mayor was Mr. Winslade Roderick, Tonyrefail, who has been a council member for over 30 years.

The first meeting of the new District Council was held in the Parish Offices, Llantrisant, on 11th January, 1895. The 60th anniversary dinner of this meeting was held on 11th January, 1955. At the final dinner of the District Council, the last Chairman Leslie Carter, Esq., J.P., presented guests with a commemorative plate bearing the Council Coat of Arms and dated 1895-1974.

At Local Government Reorganisation, Llantwit Fardre was represented on the Glamorgan County Council by:—

County Alderman William John Lewis, J.P., Beddau

County Councillor Kelvin Eason, Llantrisant

On Reorganisation, Alderman Lewis retired and penned this tribute to his loyal electorate:—

My Friends

From John O'Groats to Lands End
From Anglesey to Kent
The people that I like the best
  Are those I represent
The good, kind people of Tonteg
  And Efail Isaf too,
Church Village, Llantwit and Tynant
  I raise my hat to you.

Penycoedcae, Beddau, and Cross Inn
Llantrisant, Talbot Green,
Groesfaen and Miskin, Mwyndy Cross
And all at Pontyclun.
All at Brynsadler, Talygarn
To me you're all my friends,
That friendship I'll appreciate
Till my life's journey ends.

During a dinner to mark the end of the County Council, members were presented with a stainless steel goblet bearing the County Council Coat of Arms and dated 1889-1974.

With Local Government reorganisation, the new Mid-Glamorgan County Council came into being on 1st April, 1974, and Llantwit Fardre was represented by:—

Councillor Kelvin Eason, Llantrisant
Councillor Tudor John, Llantrisant
Councillor Luther Lodwig, Church Village
Councillor Mrs. Alice Tyrrell, Llantwit Fardre

Representing Llantwit Fardre on the new Taff-Ely Borough Council were:—

Joseph Arnold	Church Village
Leslie Boldero	Llantwit Fardre
Ieuan Hughes	Llantwit Fardre
David Bryan Millward	Church Village
Allan Frederick Watts	Tonteg

The first members of the new Llantwit Fardre Community Council were:—

Councillor	Gwyn Breeze	Tonteg
,,	Raymond Butler	Tonteg
,,	S. Douglas Davies	Tonteg
,,	Ronald S. Evans	Tonteg
,,	Mrs. Gwen Griffiths	Tonteg
,,	David Hughes, J.P.	Church Village

Councillor	D. A. Randall Isaac	Tonteg
,,	Mrs. Catherine Kemp	Tonteg
,,	E. Alun Roberts	Efail Isaf
,,	Brian Rogers	Llantwit Fardre
,,	G. Llewellyn Thomas	Church Village

The first Chairman of the Community Council was Councillor David Hughes, J.P., Church Village. Unfortunately, Councillor Hughes died early in February 1975 and as a result of the ensuing election his seat on the Council was taken by Councillor L. Lodwig, Church Village, who was already a member of Mid-Glamorgan County Council.

Before the Reform Act of 1832, the following Boroughs voted jointly to send one member to Parliament. This was the Cardiff and Contributory Borough Constituency:—

CARDIFF	LLANTRISANT	ABERAVON
SWANSEA	COWBRIDGE	KENFIG
NEATH	LOUGHOR	

In the election of 1820, the borough of Llantrisant registered 120 votes for a member. After 1832, Cardiff, Cowbridge and Llantrisant jointly returned one member, until the reform of 1918 when Llantwit Fardre was included in the Pontypridd Constituency and has been represented by the following Members of Parliament:—

Thomas Arthur Lewis Esq., M.P. 1918-1923

Thomas Isaac Mardy Jones Esq., M.P. 1923-1930—died August 1970

David Lewis Davies Esq., M.P. 1930-1938

Arthur Pearson Esq., M.P. 1938-1970—died 14th April 1980

Brynmor John Esq., M.P. 1970-

On Thursday, 7th June 1979, parishioners, in common with all living within the United Kingdom, voted for representatives to the European Parliament at present held in Strasbourg. The Labour Candidate, Mr. Winston Griffiths, a schoolmaster at Cowbridge Comprehensive School, is the first person to represent this district.

Today the parish is comprised of five main, rapidly expanding villages, Newton Llantwit, Efail Isaf, Church Village, Upper Church Village and Tonteg. The main road through the village was built by Francis Crawshay in 1839 as a way to his country house at Hensol Castle. Throughout the parish several new housing estates have been established since 1960 and are still being built. The parish has until now, kept its rural 'maerdref' character but the growth of modern industry has been in evidence within its boundaries. The result is that the district is now extensively urbanised and illustrates the current trend of movement of population downwards from valleys to the lowlands and coastal regions. Large housing estates are conspicuous and sometimes overshadow the traditional landmarks.

Since the Parish became a centre of industrial speculation in the 1820's, there has been progress down several avenues of human invention and endeavour which has showed enterprise. Industrial projects bring a movement of population and this has resulted in a pattern of action which we now know as life in our Parish.

The Centres of the Parish are the Church, Chapel, Industry and School, from which derive several social organisations with interesting and colourful events.

Llantwit Fardre has been in the forefront of the development of transport. First, the railway arrived, both the Taff Vale Company and the Barry Railway Company. When interest turned to road transport, the parish had several bus companies which formed the A.B.S. (Amalgamated Bus Service) in 1927. The only one still operating a daily service, Beddau to Pontypridd is S. A. Bebb Ltd. and who is now known here and on the Continent as Bebb International. When private transport took over, again, the Parish was the centre for Gilbern Cars, the only car produced in Wales!

Education has always played an important part in the life of this parish. Dame Schools and Circulating Schools were held here. A Colliery School was held in 1840 in stables belonging to Thomas Powell, coal speculator. In 1869, leading parishioners collected funds by public subscription to build the village school. This building is still in use for parish activities, but pupils have attended a new open-plan school since July 1974.

Other schools have been established as the population of the parish expanded but an interesting development has been in Welsh nursery education which was started in a voluntary way. This has developed over a short period to the establishment of Primary and Secondary Welsh Schools. Llantwit Fardre played the enterprising role in this work.

A Parish Library was opened in 1906 with assistance from the Carnegie Trust.

The Central Park at Church Village was established in 1939 and developed over the years. On Friday, 6th June 1980 a new Athletic Clubhouse was opened and proved a popular amenity. The Parish was honoured with a Royal Visit on Thursday, 6th November 1980 when H.R.H. Princess Anne opened the Scout and Guide Headquarters at Crown Hill.

A notable feature of Parish life is the care shown for the young, aged and infirm. When the Vestry System sustained parishioners it was the custom for the able-bodied workers to sow and reap crops in a field set aside to provide food for the less fortunate members here. Later, by 1865, The Graig Workhouse provided shelter for the needy. In 1892, a Children's Orphanage was opened at Garth Olwg and served the Community until 1964.

At Tonteg, a hospital was opened in about 1912, as an Isolation Special Care Unit because this was out in the country. Today, the hospital cares for our elderly

Senior Citizens. By 1939, East Glamorgan Hospital was built and after a period as a military hospital during World War II, was opened as a General Hospital in 1948, by Rt. Honourable Aneurin Bevan M.P., Minister of Health at the time. This continues as an important centre for health care in the Parish and for the surrounding district. A home for the Elderly was opened at Garth Olwg in 1966. Consideration for those who require special help continues today. In 1977, Maesyreglwys and Silverbrook Centres were opened to help teenage girls. In 1978, Ysgol Ty Coch opened as a special school for physically handicapped children. Senior Citizens are not forgotten. A new day centre Ty Illtyd, was opened in 1979 so that retired parishioners would have a comfortable centre to meet each day.

There is evidence throughout the history of this parish that there have always been inhabitants who have shown an active interest in matters for the well-being of their neighbours. Present day events continue in the modern age to show that parishioners have responsibility in shaping, in an imaginative and vital way, the future well-being of this place. What better symbol of faith can be found anywhere in the evidence we see on visiting the restored Parish Church, the oldest building in use in Llantwit Fardre.

Present-day parishioners have the benefit of modern science in street-lighting. This makes it possible for all to see their way when there is necessity to go about the parish at night time. Past generations only had the benefit of the parish lantern. This means the benefit of the full moon. In a rural parish like Llantwit Fardre, the moon played an important part in the lives of country folk. The moon governed the activities of farmers and market gardeners. It decided the time to plant seeds was when the moon was waxing or getting to the full. Seeds sown on the wane of the moon grew more slowly. A ring round the moon meant that wind and rain was on the way.

It was believed the meat of a pig killed when the moon

is on the wane would fry away in the pan. A pig should always be killed when the moon is waxing while an old moon in the new moon's arms—the moon was filling with water and rain. During a full moon, poachers found it necessary to get into the shade of the moon.

Country food was basic: flummery, rootcrops, meat and bread. Delicacies were made from basic foods as now. One such item was bread pudding which is popularly known as the "parish wedding cake".

Variety in diet was by seasonal and rural custom.

The photographs in this book record for us the life and times of Llantwit Fardre during a short span of history but some timeless scenic landmarks can be seen such as the Garth Mountain. This landmark is also known as Arthur's Hill because it is believed that King Arthur sleeps under it!

As you make your journey through this book, enjoying the views and meeting old friends, it is sincerely hoped that your journey Under the Parish Lantern will be a happy, nostalgic experience.

DILLWYN LEWIS.

An episode, the day before yesterday:

Twice a day, morning and evening, there is a decrease in the rate at which the traffic is moving, and it is especially noticeable in the evening when motorists travelling homeward after their day's work, plus a considerable number of passengers who are likewise longing to get home gradually come to a standstill. There is no policeman on duty, no traffic signals, and no roadman signalling his orders because road-works are ahead. What is it that brings about this subtle change? Ah, the cows! A herd of Friesians are ambling their way along from their pasture ground at one end of the village, near the East Glamorgan Hospital, to the farm near the electricity Central Control Station in the middle of the village. The cows are guided by the farmer, trapped and guarded by his dog, but they show no concern for the impatient motorist. They move from one side of the road to the other as it suits them. They come to the crossroads. They know where to turn. Haven't they done so for many a year? Now the traffic coming towards them must wait until the last cow has gone. Are they conscious of the busy highway along which they tread? I think not. The modern houses, the Old Folk's Home, the post office, the supermarket, the hotel, the adjoining betting shop, the spacious car park of the Control Station—they are no different from the allotments, the fields and the hedgerows. There is one way to the farm and they know it. Once they have gone through the gate the traffic moves again. The march of progress demands that the traffic must be kept moving, but the cows, bless them, are steadfastly maintaining the last vestige of life in a rural community.

(Church Village, W.I.
Jubilee Scrapbook 1966)

THE PARISH

Pentre'r Eglwys (Church Village) from the air 1932

My parting wish is that God should bless this Parish and that it may become an ever-increasing bulwark against materialism and the many evils of the modern world. The fine crowd of younger people who have rallied round the Church in recent years gives me cause for optimism.

E.G.M.

A Parishioner's Au Revoir 1979.

RURAL LLANTWIT FARDRE—FIFTY YEARS AGO

1

2

yright
L 18
General View, Newtown Llantwit

3

4

Copyright
N L 19
Crown, Newtown Llantwit

Copyright
N.L. 22
Garth Mountain, Newtown Llantwit.

5

6

Copyright
N.L. 23.
Church Village, Newtown Llantwit

opyright
.L.12
Church Village, Newtown Llantwit

7

8

Copyright
N.L. 20
Church Village, Newtown Llantwit

CROESCADE HOUSE

9—Squire William Perkins, J.P. lived at Croescade House until 1870. Buried at Llantrithyd Church

10—Croescade House with Samuel Evans Family on the lawn

11—Croescade House in the 1890's

12—The Mill, Efail Isaf showing members of the Pratt Family outside in 1910

13—Tŷ Mawr, Efail Isaf in 1920 *(National Library, Aberystwyth)*

14—Picturesque Hendre Scuthyn House in 1920. Hendre Scuthyn means Winter Home of the Wood Pidgeon *(National Library, Aberystwyth)*

15—Dehewid Farm, Llantwit, one of the ancient homesteads in the parish. This view taken in 1967.

16—Dehewid Fach, 1967. This farm was the home of Dic Dehewid who featured in the murder of Mallt, a servant girl who lived at Berthlwyd Farm in the eighteenth century

17—Berthlwyd Farm now a centre for sheepdog trials

18—William Henry Perkins with his family at Rhydlech Farm in 1900

19—Perkins Family at Rhydlech Farm in 1912

20—John Jenkins (John Penygroes) of Tonyrefail and his family outside Vardre Farm 1910

21—Milking time at Maendy Farm with Mr. John Williams in 1910. Miss Elizabeth Jenkins, Vicar's daughter is centre of group

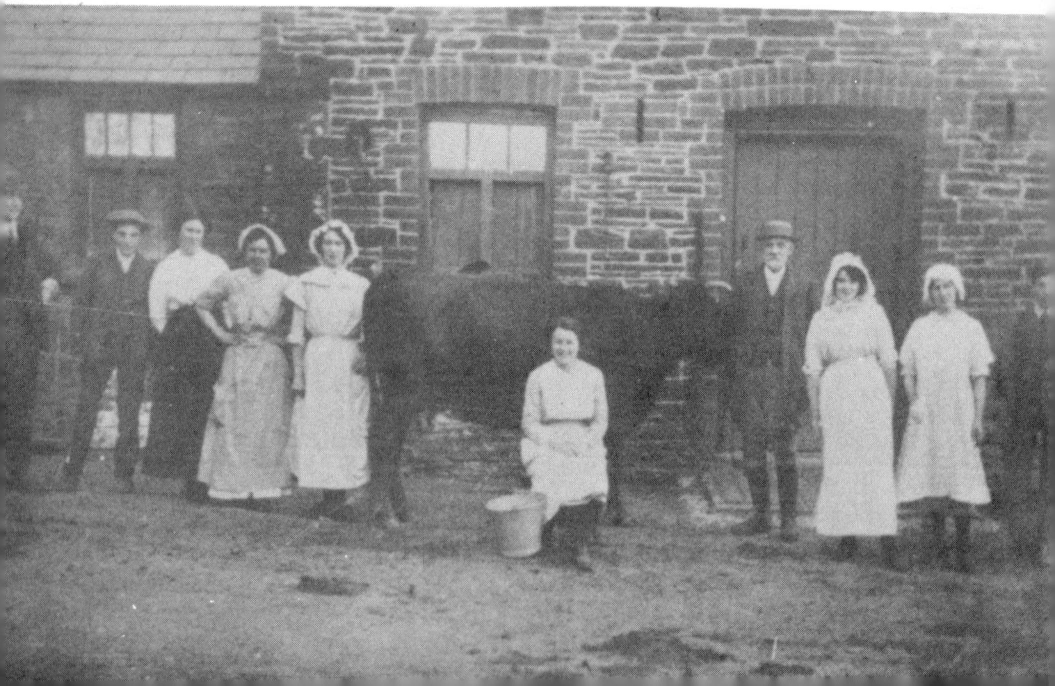

22—Maesmawr Farm, Tonteg. Mr. David Davies and his family have lived here for over 500 years. One room is known as the King's Room. It is believed Charles the First stayed here during the Civil War period

23—Celyn Farm on a fine day in 1910

24—This is Bryn Farm in 1961 prior to demolition. Hill Drive now replaces the farm. Once the home of the Williams Family, it is now remembered in Maesybryn Primary School, built on the estate in 1971

25—The year is 1865: Mrs. Jane Williams, Postmistress outside the first post office in Llantwit Fardre. The building is now incorporated into the New Inn

26—Llantwit in 1890's showing Bryn Farm in the background

27—The Railway Inn, once a busy centre of social events at Llantwit. Here we see Mr. A. Chew and Mr. J. Woodland in 1913

28—Ty'r Crwyn (Tannery). This familiar building was demolished in 1958 due to road improvements

29—Crown Hill in 1900

30—The Crown Inn in 1920

31—Bryn Terrace and St. Andrew's Church in 1924

32—Llantwit with Bryn Farm in background in 1900

33—Llantwit Station entrance and the Bush Inn in 1910

34—Llantwit Station and New Inn in 1924

35—Cross Inn, Church Village in 1913

36—Post Office, Church Village in 1900

37—Church Village in 1896

38—Cross Inn, Church Village in 1935

39—Church Village in 1946

40—Cross Inn, Church Village in 1958

41—Main road, Church Village 1914

42—The Parade, Church Village 1935

43—Main road at **Tonteg** 1935

44—Main road at Tonteg in 1920

45—Early Tonteg in 1900 showing the old Greyhound Inn (right)

46—Main road at Tonteg in 1920

47 & 48—Tomen y Clawydd (Tonteg) in 1976

49—Castell Cwrcyn (Tom Cats' Castle) Tonteg. Also known as Quarry House. The year is 1913 with the O'Brien Family and neighbours

50—The Holly Bush Hotel in 1912. Home of Nurse Jenkins who delivered a record number of babies in the parish and lived to celebrate her 100th birthday!

51—"The Holly Bush" was remodelled in 1929. Here we see it with its picturesque cottages in 1946.

52—The Hollybush today 1976

53 & 54—Two views, taken in 1976, of a noted hostelry in the parish. Now a private house, this building was once the famous "Fox & Hounds Inn"

THE PARISH CHURCH

55—Llanilltyd Faerdref in 1902 with the familiar view of St. Illtyd's Church and The Colliers Arms on the left

56—Tŷ Person Farm in 1980. This was once The Vicarage before the building of the present one in 1874

57—Rev. J. Powell Jones, B.D., Vicar of Llantrisant (1865-1883), uncle of Rev. John Jenkins, Vicar of St. Illtyd's Church (1873-1923)

58—"Ardwyn House" 1980 was built from the ruined Colliers Arms Inn on this site until the 1920's. The Colliers Arms saw many a meeting of the Parish Vestry

59—Twyn-y-Waun 1967—this house is on the site of the old "Trallwm Inn". The Inn was the venue of many a vestry meeting

60—This drawing by Rowlandson shows a Parish Vestry in 1738 like those held in Llantiwt Faerdref. Records show that meetings were held in the Church Vestry, Colliers Arms and Trallwm Inn during the eighteenth century *(Victoria and Albert Museum)*

ST. ILLTYD'S CHURCH

61—St. Illtyd's Church 1902

62—Interior, St. Illtyd's Church 1890

63—Unusual view of St. Illtyd's Church 1912

64—St. Illtyd's Church in 1925

65—Interior, St. Illtyd's Church 1925

66—Restored interior, St. Illtyd's Church 1959-60

67—Rev. Aeron A. Davies, Vicar of Llantwit Fardre 1923-1928, with the first robed choir and church members in 1924

68—Rev. David Mark, M.A., Vicar of Llantwit Fardre 1928-1949

69—Rev. Edward Vivian Dodd, B.A., Vicar of Llantwit Fardre 1949-1966

70—A Civic Service held in Festival of Britain Year 1950, Rev. E. V. Dodd, B.A., Vicar with prominent parishioners

71—A Pageant: The Church Yesterday, Today and Tomorrow produced by Rev. & Mrs. E. V. Dodd in 1952

72—A long familiar view of The Vicarage taken in 1923

73—The Vicarage, Llantwit Faerdref 1923

74—A view or The Vicarage from the vicarage field showing pigs, belonging to the Vicar, 1923

ST. ANDREW'S CHURCH, LLANTWIT

75 & 76—Opening of St. Andrew's Church, Newtown Llantwit on May 22nd, 1914

77—Opening of St. Andrew's Church, Newtown Llantwit on May 22nd, 1914

78—Interior, St. Andrew's Church, restored in celebration of its Jubilee in 1964

79—Rev. Daniel Bryant, M.A., d. 1936. Vicar of Balham, visited his native parish and dedicated the Parish War Memorial in 1919 at St. Illtyd's Church.

80—The War Memorial at St. Illtyd's Church newly restored and commemorates Service men from World War II

81—St. Illtyd's Church in 1926 when members of the Royal British Legion visited the grave of the unknown soldier

82—Rev. Arthur J. D. Williams, B.A., the present Vicar of Llantwit Fardre, with his family: Mrs. Shiela Williams, J.P. and their daughters Helen and Kathryn. The Vicar is a Freeman of Llantrisant

RESTORATION OF PARISH CHURCH 1971-74

83—Interior St. Illtyd's Church after complete rebuilding and restoration 1975

84—Interior St. Illtyd's Church, showing new organ at rear of nave 1975

85—During the period of restoration of the Parish Church, services continued at the Mission Hall. Our photograph shows the hall prepared for Sunday services

86—Crucifix above the altar in the new chapel, St. Illtyd's Church 1975

87—Interior, St. Illtyd's Church, showing entrance to new chapel 1975

88—New chapel, St. Illtyd's Church 1975

CARNIVAL TIME

89—Rev. John Jenkins with the committee, stewards and judges in 1908

90—Carnival time in the summer of 1908 in the vicarage field

91—Winning entry in the 1908 carnival held in the vicarage field

92—Fancy dress at the 1908 carnival. Miss Margaret Jenkins, Vicar's daughter is the nurse (centre)

93—Rev. John Jenkins with parishioners dressed for carnival time 1921

94—Carnival time 1921 at Church Village

95—A Biblical Presentation at the Mission Hall in the 1920's

96—A Passion Play, "By Thy Cross and Passion" presented by Rev. E. V. & Mrs. Dodd, Easter 1953

97—"The Glorious Resurrection." Rev. E. V. Dodd and Mrs. Rachel A. Dodd take part in "The Glorious Resurrection" presented at the Mission Hall in 1954

98—"Jan of Windmill Land"—an operetta presented by Rev. & Mrs. E. V. Dodd at the Mission Hall in 1952

CHAPELS IN THE PARISH

99—Bryntirion Chapel—oldest in the parish. Closed in 1961 and members worship in Bethesda

100—Efail Isaf and Tabernacl Chapel 1900

101—Bethesda Sunday School Class 1910

102—Rev. Wm. Lloyd, Minister of Bryntirion/Bethesda Chapels (1897-1937)

103—Salem Chapel in 1902, inset shows Rev. T. Richards, Minister

104—Salem Chapel Sunday School in 1946

105—Deacons and Officers of Salem Chapel, Church Village 1979

106—Rev. Caredig M. Thomas, Minister, Salem Chapel 1958-78

107—Tabanacl Chapel, Efail Isaf 1941, when it celebrated its centenary

108—Minister and Deacons in 1941, centenary year
Standing: E. Brisbane Jones, Dr. E. Parry Evans, Mrs. John Richards, David Rowlands
Sitting: David Rees, Rev. D. Stanley Jones, Rev. W. J. George

109—A fine day for working outdoors at Gwynfa Chapel with Mr. Brisbane Jones (d. August 1980), Mr. Bethel and Mr. Edward Thomas

110—Rev. J. Taihirion Davies was the first minister at Tabanacl Chapel and played a prominent part in parish affairs, who was influential in establishing Salem Chapel and in building the original village school in 1869.

111—Gwynfa Chapel, Church Village in 1923, when members of the Chapel and Sunday School presented a concert

CWM RHONDDA—INTERNATIONAL HYMN TUNE

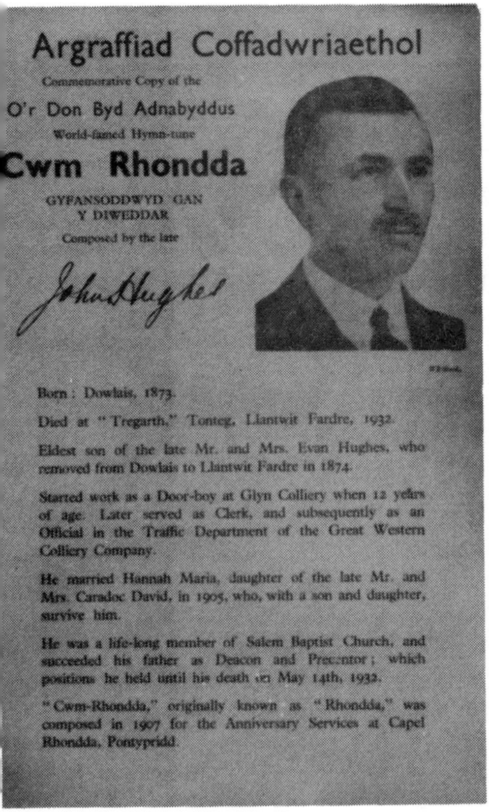

Argraffiad Coffadwriaethol

Commemorative Copy of the

O'r Don Byd Adnabyddus

World-famed Hymn-tune

Cwm Rhondda

GYFANSODDWYD GAN
Y DIWEDDAR

Composed by the late

John Hughes

Born: Dowlais, 1873.

Died at "Tregarth," Tonteg, Llantwit Fardre, 1932.

Eldest son of the late Mr. and Mrs. Evan Hughes, who removed from Dowlais to Llantwit Fardre in 1874.

Started work as a Door-boy at Glyn Colliery when 12 years of age. Later served as Clerk, and subsequently as an Official in the Traffic Department of the Great Western Colliery Company.

He married Hannah Maria, daughter of the late Mr. and Mrs. Caradoc David, in 1905, who, with a son and daughter, survive him.

He was a life-long member of Salem Baptist Church, and succeeded his father as Deacon and Precentor; which positions he held until his death on May 14th, 1932.

"Cwm-Rhondda," originally known as "Rhondda," was composed in 1907 for the Anniversary Services at Capel Rhondda, Pontypridd.

112—Cover of Commemorative Leaflet of the Composer John Hughes (1873-1932) of the international favourite, "Cwm Rhondda"

113—John Hughes in 1930 at Barry

114—Tre-Garth, Tonteg, is the house where John Hughes composed the famous tune, "Cwm Rhondda"

115—Capel Rhondda, Hopkinstown, where Cwm Rhondda was first sung in 1907

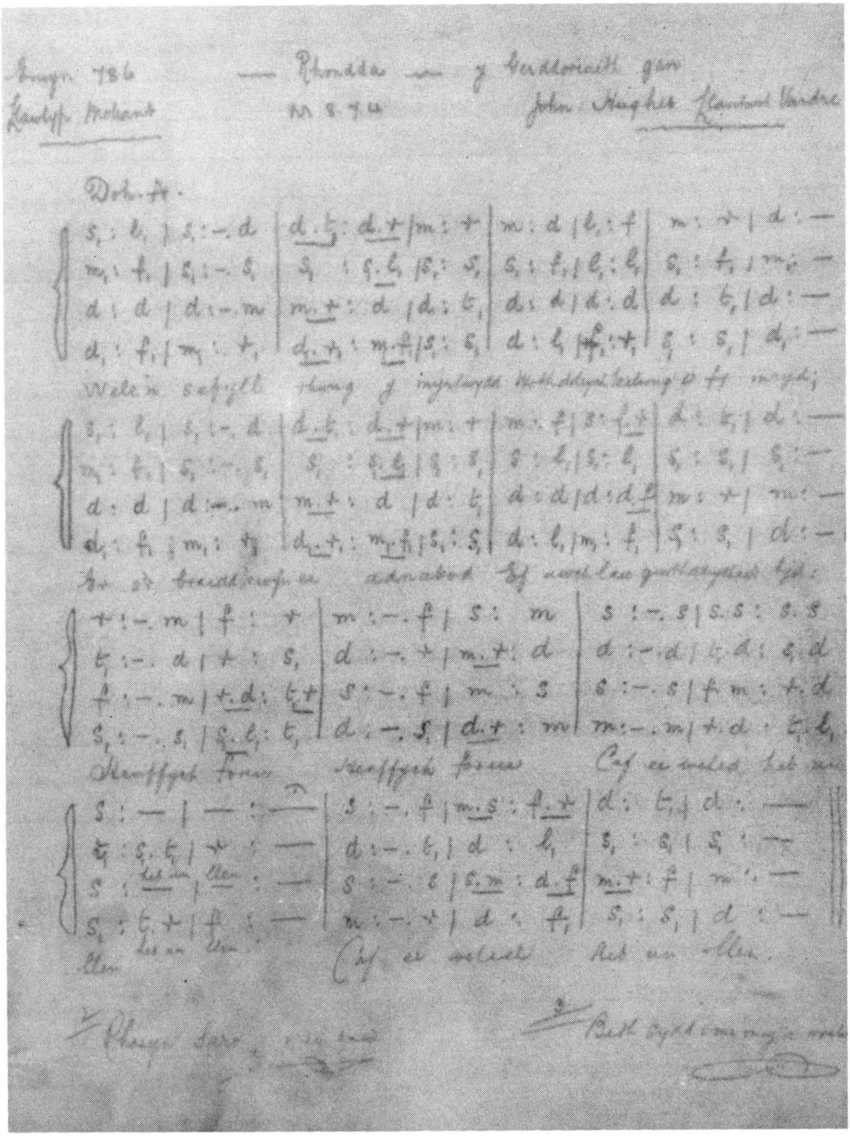

116—Photograph of original manuscript of Cwm Rhondda by John Hughes

117—Salem Welsh Baptist Chapel, Church Village

118 & 119—Memorial to John Hughes and gravestone in Salem Graveyard where the Composer lies buried

TRINITY CHAPEL, LLANTWIT

120—Rev. David John Howells, Minister, Trinity Chapel 1946-76. Here he is pictured in Mount Pleasant Chapel, Beddau, the Sister Church

Y PARCH D. J. HOWELLS
Llantwit Faerdref

Ceir llû o Weinidogion
Ar hyd a llêd ein gwlad,
Rhai gafodd gryn ddylanwad
Yn wir ar Gymru fad.
Ac un o'r rhain a haedda
Y Clod, y Parch, a'r Bri,
Yw y Parch D. J. Howells
Gweinidog Trinity.

Yn awr mae am ymddeol
A dwyn ei waith i ben,
O ddangos i'r aelodau
Y ffordd i'r Nefoedd Wen.
A chwmmwl sydd yn hofran
Uwchben fel mantell ddu,
Gan bery Poen a Tristwch
Yn Eglwys Trinity.

Mount Pleasant, a Bethesda
Sydd hefyd heddiw'n drist,
O golli un fu'n gyfrwng
Cydrhynddynt hwy a Christ.
Ai ofal gwir dihafal
Oedd amlwg o bob tu,
Ei fod Ef yn ei caru
Fel carai Trinity.

Ac i'r Parch D. J. Howells
Ai Briod hoffus llon,
Dymunwn pob hapusrwydd
Tra ar y ddaer hon.
Tra bydd Llanilltyd Faerdref,
Mewn côf yn siwr i chwi,
Fydd y Parch D. J. Howells
Gweinidog Trinity.

W. J. Lewis, J.P.
(Gwilym Llaeron)

121—Trinity Chapel in 1914 when members and Sunday School scholars presented the first concert in their new Church

122—Trinity Chapel built in 1913 and celebrated its jubilee in 1963

123—Rev. John Badham and Chapel members at tea in Llantwit Road in the 1930's

124—Rev. D. J. Howells and Mrs. Howells with members of Trinity Chapel during the Jubilee Supper 1963. Note the cake baked as a model of Trinity Chapel

125—Forest House, Treforest when it was the home of Francis Crawshay, son of Merthyr Iron Master, William Crawshay. In 1910, the house became the School of Mines and now is the Polytechnic of Wales. *(Glamorgan Archive Service)*

126—Francis Crawshay

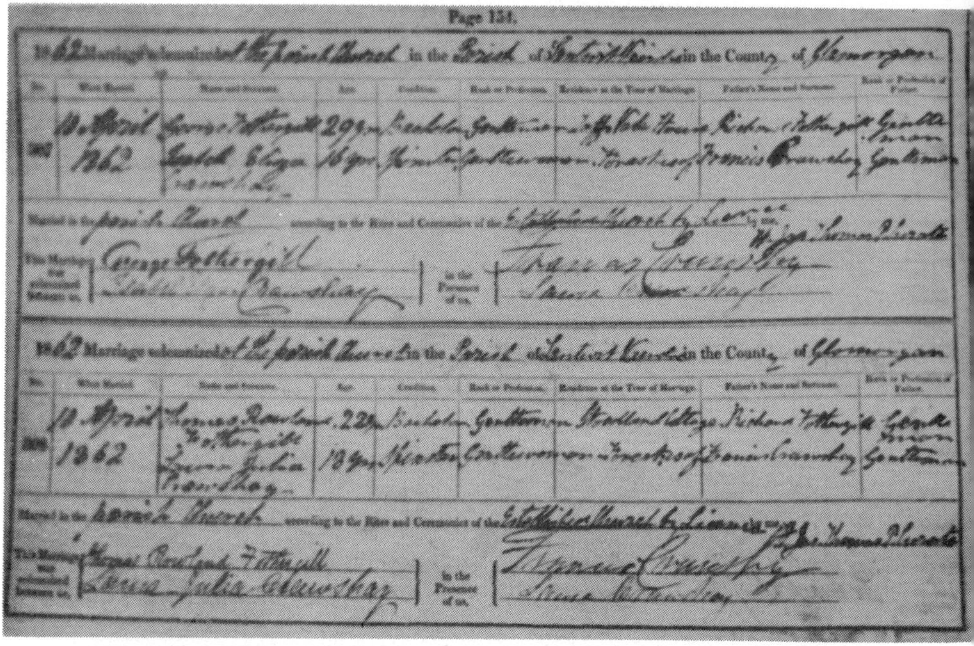
Page 154.

127—A double wedding at St. Illtyd's Church on 10th April, 1862, showing the daughters of Francis Crawshay married the sons of Rowland Fothergill

128—Colliery surveyors at the New School of Mines, Treforest, in 1910

129—Thomas Powell 1797-1864, coal speculator in Llantwit Fardre and Tynant and founder of the Powell Duffryn organisation. *(Powell Duffryn Ltd.)*

130—A sketch of Ida House, Tynant, showing the Colliery Offices of the Charles Pit and where Thomas, son of Thomas Powell, lived before being killed by cannibals while on holiday in Abyssinia in 1872

131

132

133—An interesting view of Bryn Colliery, Llantwit in 1900. Now the site of Tupperware Ltd.

134—Dehewid Colliery, Llantwit, in 1902 showing workmen

135—Llest Colliery, Llantwit, 1906

136—Dismantling Penrhiw Colliery in 1970. The frame and headgear was made of wood

137—Mr. Creswell Richards in the engine house at Penrhiw Colliery 1970

138—Cwm Farm, a rural retreat in 1900

139—Cwm Colliery, Wednesday, 13th October, 1909. Cutting the first turf

140—Cwm Colliery sinkers, 1912

141—Cwm Colliery—installing the cages 1912, is Mr. Hubert Davies

142—Cwm Colliery workmen, 1912

143—Original Cwm Colliery 1912

144—Screens 1912

145 & 146—Engine House, Cwm Colliery, 1912

147 & 148—Engine House, Cwm Colliery, 1912

149—Fitting Shop, Cwm Colliery, 1912

150—Engine House showing outlet of fan, 1912

151 & 152—Cwm Colliery—views underground, 1912

153 & 154—Cwm Colliery—views underground, 1912

155—Cwm Colliery—views underground, 1912

THE LIZZIE DOUBLE PARTING
(Cwm Colliery)

When I was at Cwm Colliery
I earned an honest living
Whilst working for the N.C.B.
On Lizzie's Double Parting.

And though I tackled various jobs
My main job was repairing,
And many Steel Rings I put up
On Lizzie's Double Parting.

Sometimes the Engine I would drive
My mate would do the riding,
And many journeys we dispatched
From Lizzie's Double Parting.

And many narrow squeaks we had
On Robert's Hardheading,
When trams would often run away
From Lizzie's Double Parting.

The little mice I entertained
With my melodious singing
And we became the best of friends
On Lizzie's Double Parting.

And now as I am getting old
And as my life is fading,
Down Memory Lane my thoughts
will stroll
To Lizzie's Double Parting.

W. J. Lewis, J.P.
(Gwilym Llaeron)

156—Sinking the shaft—Cwm Colliery, 1909-10

157—Meeting point of tunnel linking Cwm and Coedely Collieries in 1957

158—Rescue Team, Cwm Colliery, 1918

159—Rescue Team, Cwm Colliery, 1920's

160—St. John Ambulance Brigade, Cwm Colliery, 1922

161—Mr. Jack Pryce and fitters at Cwm Colliery in 1950's. Mr. Trefor Pryce now an engineer with N.C.B., son of the chief fitter, is also in the picture

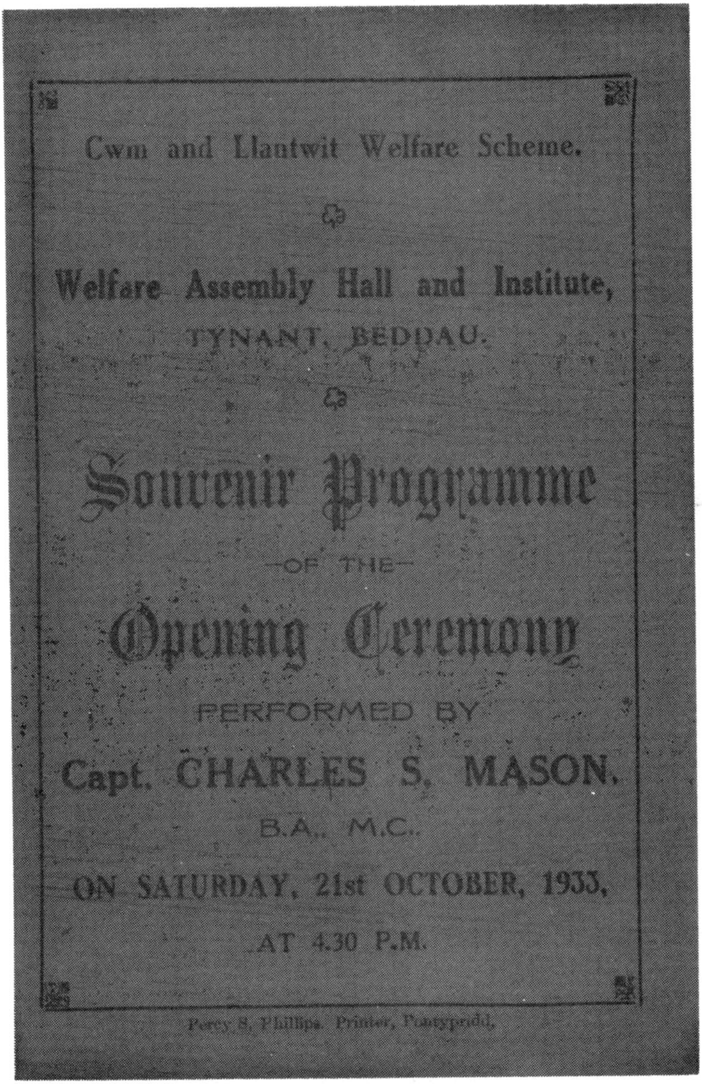

Cwm and Llantwit Welfare Scheme.

Welfare Assembly Hall and Institute,

TYNANT, BEDDAU.

Souvenir Programme

—OF THE—

Opening Ceremony

PERFORMED BY

Capt. CHARLES S. MASON,

B.A., M.C.,

ON SATURDAY, 21st OCTOBER, 1933,

AT 4.30 P.M.

Percy S. Phillips, Printer, Pontypridd.

162—Cover of Souvenir Programme of Opening, Welfare Hall

163—Laying Foundation Stone, Welfare Hall, **Beddau**, by D. L. Davies, M.P. on 11th August, **1932**

164—Welfare Committee and guests at **Opening** of Welfare Hall, Beddau, on Saturday, 21st October, 1933

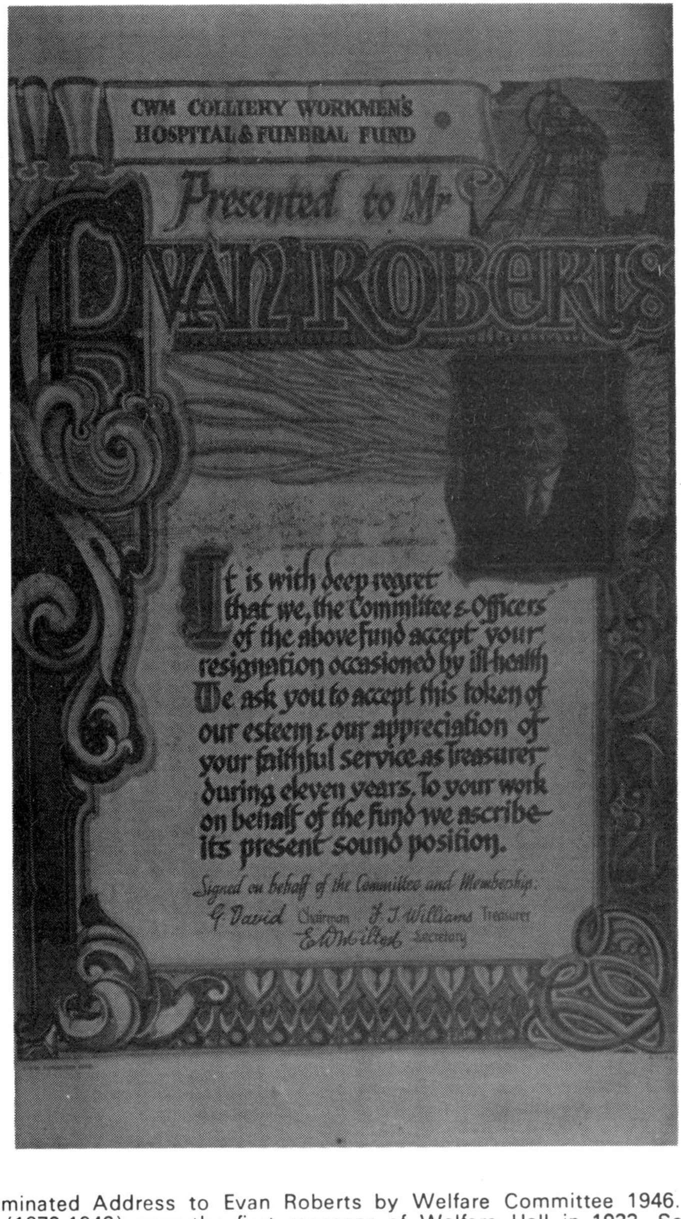

165—Illuminated Address to Evan Roberts by Welfare Committee 1946. Mr. Evan Roberts (1878-1946) was the first manager of Welfare Hall in 1933. Secretary to Welfare Committee 1924-46

166—Gaiety Cinema Staff, 1935. Richard Roberts, projectionist, assistant projectionist and Mrs. May Keohane, usherette

167—Welfare Hall in 1935 as Gaiety Cinema

168—Cwm Lodge Officers, 30th May, 1947, on the occasion of two members of the Lodge being Chairman of Llantrisant and Llantwit Fardre R.D.C. and Pontypridd U.D.C.
L. to R.—Treasurer, W. J. Lewis; Councillor Ivor Jacobs (Llantrisant); Gwilym David, Chairman; Councillor Herbert Gardiner (Pontypridd) and Thomas Mason, Secretary

169—Representatives of Cwm Lodge on Welfare Committee with Council Chairmen, 30th May, 1947

170—Cwm Lodge Committee on 22nd June, 1947, showing Lodge and Management. Colliery Manager, Mr. D. L. Jones, in centre of front row

171—Councillor William John Lewis, J.P., Chairman Llantrisant & Llantwit Fardre Rural District Council with Cwm Welfare Committee in 1956

172—Cwm Welfare Beauty Queen and Lodge Committee in 1949

173—Cwm Colliery Canteen Committee, 1941-52

174—Officers and Committee of the Cwm Colliery Hospital and Funeral Fund, 1947

175—Cwm Lodge Officials with their banner on Miners' Gala Day in Cardiff

176—Prior to the 1946 National Insurance Act the 1911 Insurance Act, promoted by David Lloyd George, provided social security for ordinary people by Friendly Societies. An important society in this district was the Bristol, West of England and South Wales Provident Society. The agent was Mr. E. Evan Roberts (1878-1946), Beddau, who served the society 1910-1946. Assisting at Beddau Agency 220, distributing insurance cards and sickness benefit, was Evan Roberts' wife, Mrs. Priscilla Roberts (1877-1963). Our photo shows her celebrating her eightieth birthday on 27th February, 1957. She played a prominent part in welfare services during the depressed 1920's and 30's

177—Mr. Pryce Hardwick, colliery sinker (1865-1949) and parish councillor

178—Modern Cwm Colliery and Coking Plant

179—Sgt. John Frankton in 1940. Came to the Cwm Colliery in 1931 and retired from the Force on 1st January, 1947

180—Police Sergeant E. Welsley who served at Cwm Colliery 1946-1963

181—Cwm Welfare Committee with Councillor William John Lewis, J.P., Chairman Llantrisant & Llantwit Fardre Rural District Council 1956-57

182—Presentation to Mr. Gwilym David on the occasion of receiving the B.E.M. in the Honours List. Photograph shows Mrs. David and Mr. Arthur Pearson, M.P. (left)

SOUTH WALES ELECTRICITY BOARD
UPPER BOAT POWER STATION 1902-1976

183—Ty'r Nell Farm, centre of religious meetings in the parish. The boy in the photograph is Mr. John Morgan now farming at Pontypridd. The farmhouse was demolished to make way for the new electric works. It was at this farmhouse that the first religious meetings were held in the 1730's which led to the establishment of Bryntirion Chapel in 1746

184—Upper Boat Electricity Power Station b. 1902

185—Haymaking at the Power Station field in 1905

186—Upper Boat Power Station before demolition in 1976

187—Demolition of Upper Boat Power Station 1976

188—The year is 1910, the Vicar, Rev. John Jenkins and his wife prepare to travel through the parish in the popular form of transport, pony and trap

189—The Crown Hill Blacksmith, Charlie Tuck in 1920. There were several blacksmith shops in the parish when horse-drawn vehicles were popular

190—Transport in "The Woodlands", 1928

191—Llantwit in 1920's, showing horse-drawn transport

192—Church Village Cross in 1900 showing Mr. Daniel Bryant with his transport he used for deliveries around the parish

193—Salem Lane, Church Village, a picturesque rural retreat during the snows in 1973

194—The tranquil heyday—It's a long while since Llantwit Vardre Railway Station closed . . . but here it is in its heyday early in the century. Not a very active heyday, on the particular day the photograph was taken, mind you. But at least there were real trains steaming through, boarded by real passengers paying fares that were at some reasonable level. All that's changed now. The passengers have gone . . . the trains have gone . . . and elsewhere the fares have rocketed

195—Llantwit Station staff in the 1920's

196—Efail Isaf Station — the Barry Railway before 1922

197—Efail Isaf Station (Barry line), Mr. Maurice Charles Tottle, Stationmaster 1930-46. Station closed 1958 and demolished. Private house now stands on the site. The young porter is Mr. Hywel Tottle in 1932

198—Church Village Railway Station in its heyday in 1920's and 1930's. It was closed in 1958. The station is now used by a firm

199—The year is 1909 when Beddau Halt railway platform was opened (Taff Vale line). The picture shows the construction of the road leading to the station entrance. The station was closed in 1951

200—Palmer's bus on the Pontypridd/Beddau route in 1921. This was one of the first buses of several enterprising persons to bring public transport to the parish

201—The photograph shows the first bus of Edwards Bros., Beddau, in 1923. In 1927 Mr. George Edwards joined four other concerns to form the amalgamated bus service on the Beddau/Pontypridd route

202—Edwards Bros. bus on the stand at Beddau Square in 1937. The driver is Mr. Cyril Edwards. This Bus Company is still in business directed by Mr. Alvis Edwards

203—The photograph shows Cox's buses on the stand at Pontypridd in 1924. Buses like these ran on the Beddau/Pontypridd/Pontyclun route

204—Gray's bus taking a special outing in 1920's. Note: Model of Charlie Chaplin

205—Opportunities abounded for enterprising persons to set up business. Here we see Mr. Gerwyn Mustow who spent a lifetime in business, latterly at the Transport Cafe on the Llantwit main road

206—Stop me and buy one!—That was the cry. This is a picture to stir the memory of all who like ice-cream. Taken at Tynant in 1922

207—Welsh Hills Mineral Waters in 1929. This began the convenient house to house system of selling. Albert Thomas, Llantwit, was employed by Thomas & Evans Ltd., the well-known family grocers who pioneered 'Corona' Mineral Waters

208—Thomas & Evans Ltd., Porth change over from horse-powered transport to motorised vehicles in 1929. Albert Thomas, Llantwit, stands near the new vehicle.

209—The year is 1928, Mr. Clifford Crook with his first vehicle. He is still in business at Holly Bush Garage, Church Village, on the site of Gray's Bus Company which closed in 1956

210—Car service in 1922. The drivers are two well-known personalities of the parish, Mr. Price Thomas and Mr Alfred Gardener

211—A familiar sight throughout the parish was Mr. Price Thomas, Greengrocer. Here he is in 1928 with his first mode of transport

212—Here is Mr. Price Thomas still in business with Mr. Dick Morgan in 1964

213—Producing the new Invader Mark VI Car at Gilbern Factory in 1975

The Fabulous

GILBERN

The only car built entirely in Wales

HAND-BUILT LUXURY FOR FOUR PERSONS

Cars are finished to customers' individual specifications

•

DUAL BRAKING SYSTEM
Fully adjustable reclining seats
3-LITRE V6 ENGINE
giving vivid acceleration — and
A TOP SPEED OF OVER 100 m.p.h.

•

GILBERN SPORTS CAR
LIMITED
PENTWYN WORKS, LLANTWIT FARDRE
Tel. Newtown Llantwit 571

215—Mr. Bernard Friese and Mr. Giles Smith, founders of Gilbern

216—How's this for a museum piece? It's an example of old transport, circa 1972. Eight years old and ready for the museum—Dr. Jones displays the latest historical exhibit.

An immaculate version of a Gilbern—Wales' only production car—is to go on show at Cardiff's Industrial and Maritime Museum.

The museum have bought a completely overhauled 1972 model for their collection, and it will go on show early next month during a special open day.

The car was specially restored in London before being handed over to the museum this week. It was brought down by lorry to their workshops in the city's docks area.

The cars, which were produced at Llantwit Fardre from 1962 until the company went broke in 1974, are becoming increasingly rare—and the museum's assistant director, Dr. Stuart Owen Jones, decided to acquire one while the vehicles were still available.

"The Gilbern company produced about 1,000 over the years, and as they were the only cars ever made in volume in Wales we felt it would be a suitable addition to our collection of old vehicles," said Dr. Jones.

"Although this car is relatively modern, today's products do become tomorrow's museum pieces and we are very lucky to have such a good low-mileage example."

Loft prototype

Although Dr. Jones preferred not to discuss how much the museum paid for the car, experts say the market price for Gilberns ranges between £2,500 and £3,000—if you can find one for sale.

The idea for the Gilbern was hatched in the mid-1950's by butcher Giles Smith and salesman Bernard Friese, both motoring enthusiasts. They combined the first letters of their names, and in 1957 produced the first prototype Gilbern in a one-roomed garage loft in Llantwit Fardre.

They later took over factory premises and went into commercial production. After initial success the company became dogged by financial problems and were wound up in 1974 with debts of £90,000. A number of attempts to revive the company failed.

(Reproduced from *South Wales Echo*, 14th November, 1980)

217—Doctor's Corner in 1924 giving a view of the original doctor's surgery alongside Dr. Washington Evans' house. Dr. Evans practised in the parish from 1921 until 1955 when Dr. James Wakelin, a partner since 1953, took over the practice

218—Road repairs 1924 style. Dr. Evans' surgery is in the background

219—Road repairs in the parish

220—Under construction! A familiar sight in the parish during the present time. Here we see Holly Bush Villas being built in 1928

221—Craftsmen all pause to have their photograph taken at Holly Bush Villas in 1928

222—Llantwit Fardre School Board—School Mistresses at Pontypridd, 1903

223—Llantwit Faerdref School Board—School Masters at Pontypridd, 1903

224—Garth Olwg Children's Homes. Our photograph shows Master and Mistress, Mr. and Mrs. Targett and Mr. and Mrs. Axtell. The homes opened in 1892 and finally closed in 1964

225—Treilltyd School where all children in Garth Olwg attended until at eleven years of age, pupils attended Beddau Senior School (Bryn Celynnog). The school closed in 1955. The buildings are still used as Llanilltud Faerdref Infants' School

226—Mr. Curwen Griffiths, Beddau, Headteacher from 1948 until 1955 when the school was closed

227—Mr. Curwen Griffiths, Headteacher and staff at Treilltyd School, 1955

228—Llantwit Fardre School Board, 1903. Our photograph shows Mr. Daniel Bryant (with beard) and Rev. John Jenkins, Vicar of Llantwit Fardre (right seated)

229—Mr. Lewis Williams c. 1880 with his daughter. He was Headmaster at the Board School 1876-1911

230—Our photograph shows the last Board of Governors of Llantrisant Secondary Schools before local government re-organisation in April, 1974

231—This photograph records the last members of Pontypridd & Llantrisant Divisional Executive in April, 1974 before local government re-organisation. The Executive had governed the schools since it was established in April, 1945

LLANILLTUD FAEDREF SCHOOL
(BRITISH SCHOOL 1869)

232—Llantwit British School opened in 1869. This is the earliest photograph (1876) showing Lewis Williams, Headteacher, staff and pupils. Mr. Williams retired in 1911 and is well-known for a book, "Mallt o Duffryn", he wrote relating to life in Llantwit Faerdref in 1912

233—This unusual photograph shows staff and pupils on the retirement of the

234—On 1st July, 1974, pupils moved into the new village school built on the
Faer

ner, Mr. William Chubb in 1922. Mr. Chubb had been Headteacher since 1911

style. Here we see Mr. Arthur Williams, Headteacher with pupils of Llanilltud School

LLANILLTUD FAEDREF SCHOOL THROUGH THE YEARS

235—The year is 1876. Mr. Lewis Williams, Headteacher and pupils

236—The class of 1910 with their teacher

237—The year is 1949. Mr. Llewellyn Richards, Headteacher and Miss Winnie Griffiths

238—Staff photograph marking the retirement of the Headteacher, Mr. William Chubb in 1922

239—The year is 1933. Mr. Llewellyn Richards, Headteacher, with his staff

240—Festival Year 1951. Mr. William Morgan and his staff

241—A summer's day in 1902 when Schoolmistresses posed for this photograph

242—Pre-World War I and the boys show a fashion in flat caps c. 1910

243—The year is 1932 when this delightful photograph recorded happy faces with their teacher and Mr. Llewellyn Richards

244—Pupils during pre-1930's

245—Pupils during the 1930's

246—Flashback : Installing central heating in the British School in 1923

247 & 248—School meals are now a part of the school day. These photographs show Llanilltud Faerdref pupils having lunch in 1941. Meals were first supplied by the headteacher and the system was visited and copied by other authorities. Church Village became the blueprint for the future after World War II ended in 1945

249—Mr. William Davies and staff of Llanilltud Faerdref Junior School, 1978

250—And into the 1980's : Pupils of the fourth year with Headmistress Mrs. H. H. George

LLANILLTUD FAERDREF INFANTS' SCHOOL

251—Llanilltud Faerdref Infants' Class in the 1950's

252—Miss Elizabeth Roberts and staff of the Infants' School in 1955

253—Infant pupils with their teacher Miss Dorothy Thomas and Headmistress, Miss Elizabeth Roberts in 1955

254—Infant pupils, Llanilltud Faerdref Infants' School 1962. with Mrs. Gwen Jones who became Headmistress until 1972

255—In 1958, the Infants' School moves to Garth Olwg. Here we see Miss Nest Mathews and her staff in the grounds in 1958

YSGOL GYNRADD CYMRAEG GARTH OLWG

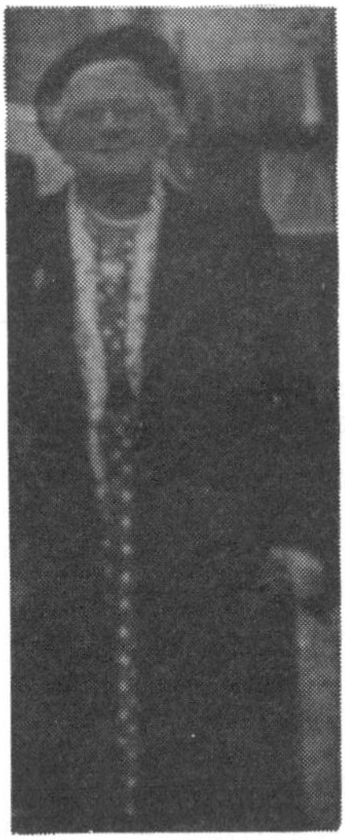

256—Miss Margaret Rosser (1882-1967), Efail Isaf, founder of the Welsh Nursery School Movement

257—Welsh Nursery Class founded in 1959, seen here in the Parish Hall with Miss Winnie Griffiths and Mrs. Harte in 1960's

258—This harp belonged to Miss Margaret Rosser. Here it is played by Miss Elin Morse, with Nerys Wyn Davies in 1979

259—Miss Rosser in her bardic robes "Megan Illtyd"

260—The first Headteacher Mr. Vivian Harries, B.A., with his staff when the school opened in 1966

261—This happy photograph records the Headteacher Mr. Vivian Harries, BA, with his staff in Jubilee Year 1977

262—Garth Olwg's successful team in H.T.V's. Quiz 'Stesion Cantamil': Nicholas Davies, Gareth Bebb, Ian Christopher, Ian Daniel; the year 1976

GWAUNCELYN SCHOOLS, TONTEG

263—Gwauncelyn Primary School opened January, 1967

264—Our photograph shows first days in a new school with Mr. E. Lock, Headteacher and Miss Eluned Thomas who became Headteacher of the Infants' School in 1969

265—Gwauncelyn Infant's School in 1978. Our photograph shows Miss Jean Singer, Headmistress, with her staff

266—A red letter day for Gwauncelyn Junior School when their swimming pool was declared open on 16th April, 1977, by County Councillor Philip Squires, Chairman of the Education Committee and Mr. John Brace, M.A., Director of Education

MAESYBRYN COUNTY PRIMARY SCHOOL, LLANTWIT

267—The first Headteacher, Mr. Dillwyn Lewis and staff of Maesybryn School which opened, September, 1971

268—The photograph shows the whole school with staff and headteacher when the school opened in 1971

269—Scene of official opening of Maesybryn School

270—Ystradbarwig School was held in Trinity Chapel 1925 to 1931. Our photograph shows pupils in Infant Department in February, 1928

271—Scene during the Official Opening Ceremony on Thursday, 18th May, 1972

272—County Councillor William John Lewis, J.P., officially opened Maesybryn School watched by the County Surveyor and the Headteacher on Thursday, 28th May, 1972

273—The Official Opening of Maesybryn School is commemorated by a plaque. Here we see Mrs. Ann Lewis unveiling the plaque on opening day, watched by County Alderman John Haydn Thomas, J.P., County Alderman William John Lewis, J.P. and the Headteacher Mr. Dillwyn Lewis on Thursday, 18th May, 1972

274—Ten years on . . . The Headteacher Mr. Dillwyn Lewis and members of staff at Maesybryn County Primary School, which celebrates its tenth anniversary in September, 1981

BRYN CELYNNOG COMPREHENSIVE SCHOOL, BEDDAU

275—Beddau Senior School with Mr. D. R. Dawkins, M.Sc., Headmaster, with his staff in 1932

276—The year is 1933 with plus-fours in fashion. Mr. D. R. Dawkins, MSc., Headmaster with his staff. Mr. R. W. Francis (seated extreme left) became Headmaster of Bryn Celynnog Secondary School 1960-1970

277—Bryn Celynnog Comprehensive School opened September, 1972. Here we see Mr. J. G. Lloyd, B.Sc., Headmaster and his staff

278—Our photograph shows members of the Bryn Celynnog School Band which has brought honour to the school on many occasions

YOUNG PARISHIONERS CONTINUE OLD TRADITIONS

279—Jubilee Year 1977 when pupils performed, "A Handful of Songs", a programme of 25 years of popular music in celebration of the Jubilee of Queen Elizabeth II, November, 1977

280—Our photograph shows full cast of "The Melodies Linger On" performed at Maesybryn Primary School, Llantwit in November, 1978

281—Martin Samuel, a young parishioner, continuing an old tradition by greeting the audience at Maesybryn Primary School during a programme of Olde Tyme Music Hall in 1978. He was only 10 years old. A moment to be cherished by all who witnessed his performance

282—1979 was designated the International Year of the Child. Our photograph shows a scene from "Along the Yellow Brick Road" at Maesybryn Primary School. The concert consisted of characters from children's literature presented as a musical

ST. DAVID'S DAY TRADITION

283—St. David's Day celebrations are traditional in schools. Here we see Infant pupils dressed in Welsh costume on 1st March, 1980, at Maesybryn Primary School, Llantwit

284—St. David's Day 1980 at Maesybryn Primary School with Junior pupils in costume to present St. David—this is your life, T.V. style

285—Sportsday at Maesybryn School, 15th June, 1978, when the school football team were presented with commemorative plaques to mark winning the Llantrisant District League Cup. Our photograph shows Mr. T. L. Williams, Sports Master; Mr. Fred Pethard (Cardiff City A.F.C.); and Mr. Dillwyn Lewis, Headteacher. The plaques were presented by Llantwit Faerdref Community Council

286—A visit to Maesybryn School, Llantwit by Vice-Chairman Llewellyn Thomas, Communitly Council, to present the David Hughes Memorial Cup and Llantwit Faerdref Community Cup to teams of the school on 10th April, 1979

287—1979 Sports Personality of the Year. First award made to David Stanton

288—Crown Hill Ladies' Guild President Mrs. Shirley Emmanuel and Secretary Mrs. Dainty present a shield to Mr. Dillwyn Lewis, Headteacher, Maesybryn School for use of pupils in November, 1978

289—The Chairman of the Llantwit Fardre Community Council, Councillor Brian Rogers presents Mr. Dillwyn Lewis, Headteacher, Maesybryn County Primary School, Llantwit, on Thursday, 4th December, 1980 with a silver cup to be used as a sports trophy and competed for annually by pupils of the school

290—The Phoenix Karate Club, Crown Hill, Llantwit. Trophy winners 1980. Mr. Norman Holloway is the leader

PONTYCLUN TEACHERS' ASSOCIATION (N.U.T.)
FOUNDED JANUARY 1898

291—Officers of the Pontyclun Teachers' Association with Mr. Dewi G. Bonner elected Junor Vice-President of the National Unoin of Teachers 1975. Our photograph shows Mr. Gwilym Moses, Secretary; Mr. Roy Davies, President; Mr. Dewi G. Bonner; Mr. Geraint Jenkins, Vice-President; Mr. Dillwyn Lewis, Treasurer

292—Dewi G. Bonner, President National Union of Teachers 1978 at his desk, Blackpool Conference

293—Mr. Dewi G. Bonner with Mrs. Bonner and members of the Pontyclun & Mid Glamorgan Teacher's Association at Blackpool, March, 1978 attending a dinner given by Welsh Delegates to the Conference

293A—On Thursday, 29th January, 1981 Mrs. Alice Hague (President of the Pontyclun Teachers' Association) presented Mr. Dewi G. Bonner with an illuminated address recording 'the best thanks of members of the Pontyclun Teachers' Association' for his many services on behalf of teachers in the district and nationally. Mr. E. Lock (Vice-President) and Mrs. Margaret Bonner also appear in the photograph

294—Mr. Dewi G. Bonner addressing the Scarborough Conference 1979

295—Scarborough Conference 1979, Mr. Dewi G. Bonner receiving the best thanks of Conference and presented with a memento of being President by the in-coming President Mr. Jim Murphy

LLANTRISANT & LLANTWIT FAERDREF R.D.C.
1894-1974

296—Members of the Llantrisant & Llantwit Faerdref Rural District Council in 1952-53

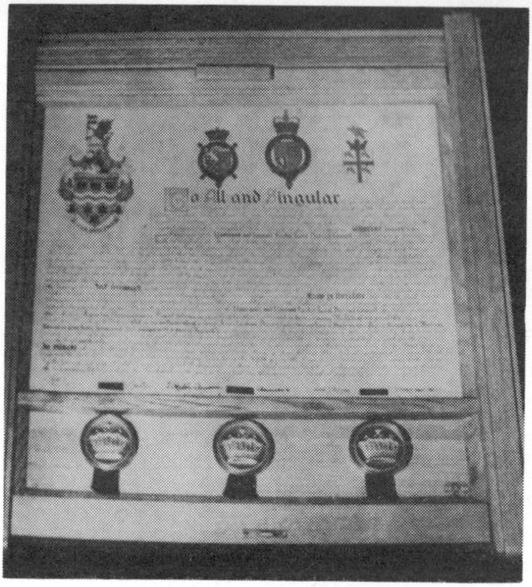

297—Grant of Armorial Bearings to Llantrisant & Llantwit Faerdref R.D.C. 1957

298—Insignia of the Chairman Llantrisant & Llantwit Faerdref R.D.C.

299—Civic Sunday, 17th June, 1956 at St. Michael & All Angels Church, Beddau, for Chairman William John Lewis, J.P. (centre), Llantrisant & Llantwit Faerdref R.D.C. with Councillor John, Chairman Stroud R.D.C.,Glos. and Councillor Joe Lawrence, Chairman Ogmore & Garw R.D.C.

ELIZABETH THE SECOND

by the Grace of God of the United Kingdom of Great Britain and Northern Ireland and of Our other Realms and Territories Queen, Head of the Commonwealth, Defender of the Faith:

TO ALL TO WHOM THESE PRESENTS SHALL COME, GREETING!

WHEREAS certain new local government areas known as districts have been established by the Local Government Act 1972:

AND WHEREAS a Petition praying for the grant of a Charter conferring upon the district of Taff-Ely the status of a borough has been presented unto Us by the council of the said district:

AND WHEREAS We are pleased by the advice of Our Privy Council to grant a Charter for such purpose.

NOW THEREFORE KNOW YE that We, by virtue of Our Prerogative Royal and in pursuance of the Local Government Act 1972 and of all other powers and authorities enabling Us in that behalf, have granted and declared and by these Presents do grant and declare that the district of Taff-Ely shall have the status of a borough.

This Our Charter shall not take effect before the first day of April, One thousand nine hundred and seventy-four.

IN WITNESS whereof We have caused these Our Letters to be made Patent.

WITNESS Ourself at Westminster the *twenty seventh* day of *February* in the *twenty-third* year of Our Reign.

Borough of Taff Ely Charter granted 1974

300—Taff Ely Charter

301—Llantrisant & Llantwit Fardre R.D.C., 1974: Back row—H. S. Davies; R. W. Thomas; K. Williams, Dep. Treasurer; J. Gardines, Dep. Surveyor; W. R. Jacob; S. Balby; T. John; J. A. Copeland; R. J. Brown, Treasurer. Middle row—R. A. Huxton, Dep. Clerk; T. J. Hopkins, Surveyor; S. G. Flower; D. J. Harrison; K. Roderick, K. Ponting; I. Hughes; S. Mason, P.H.Ins. Front row—Dr. Eileen G. Watkins, M.O.H.; Dr. W. Moody Jones; Mrs. A. G. Herbert; R. J. Selwood, Vice-Chairman; L. L. Carter, J.P., Chairman; W. J. Maddocks, Clerk; T. W. Roderick; R. Cox

THE LLANTWIT FAERDREF PARISH COUNCIL 1894-1974 BECAME THE COMMUNITY COUNCIL IN 1974

302—Llantwit Faerdref Parish Council in 1946 recording many well-known parishioners. Mrs. Phillips was the Clerk to the Parish Council who met in the Carnegie Library

303—Llanilltud Faerdref Community Council with their Chairman Councillor Douglas S. Davies and Mr. Haydn Jones, Clerk, during Jubilee Year 1977

4—The original Chairman's ain of Office for the Parish uncil, presented by Mr. W. Dallimore

305—The Chain of Office of Chairman of the Community Council used during the present time

306—A Civic Sunday at Bethesda Chapel, Llantwit for Parish Council Chairman, Councillor Thomas Jones, 19th July, 1959

SOCIAL SERVICES IN THE PARISH

307—The Almshouses in 1910 showing Daniel and Jane Davies, Mrs. Elizabeth Jenkins' daughter lived here until 1968. The cottages had existed since 1700

308—The Almshouses modernised into a single cottage, derelict since 1970

309—This photograph taken outside The Graig, Pontypridd Union Workhouse, shows the Board of Guardians in 1903

310—The Hospital Management Committee outside the old Graig Hospital, Pontypridd in 1965 when it was demolished to make way for the modern Dewi Sant Hospital

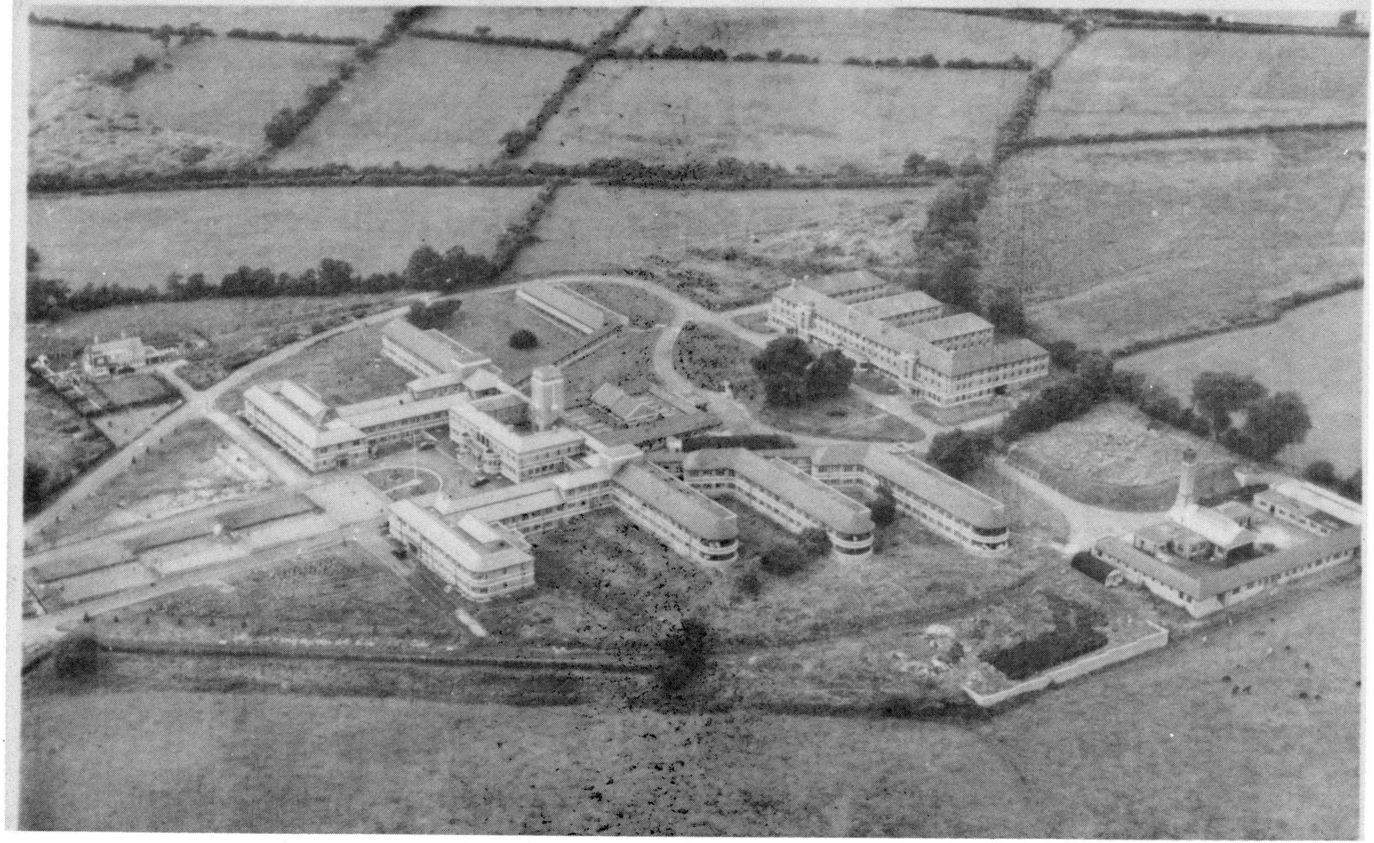

311—East Glamorgan Hospital b. 1938/9 and used as a R.A.F. Services Unit during World War II. Since it was opened by Aneurin Bevan, Minister of Health in 1948, it has developed into a major hospital in South Wales

312—Views of the recent Maesyreglw
in

313—Ysgol Tŷ Coch, Tonteg, a school for mentally handicapped children, opened in April, 1978

rook Community Home which opened
977

314—A red letter day when Ysgol Tŷ Coch was officially opened on Thursday, 17th September, 1979. Our photograph shows County Councillor D. Macdonald, Mrs. E. Bazanko (Headmistress), County Councillor Luther Lodwig, County Councillor Philip Squires, Mrs. Lodwig and Mr. Aylwyn Jones (Director of Education)

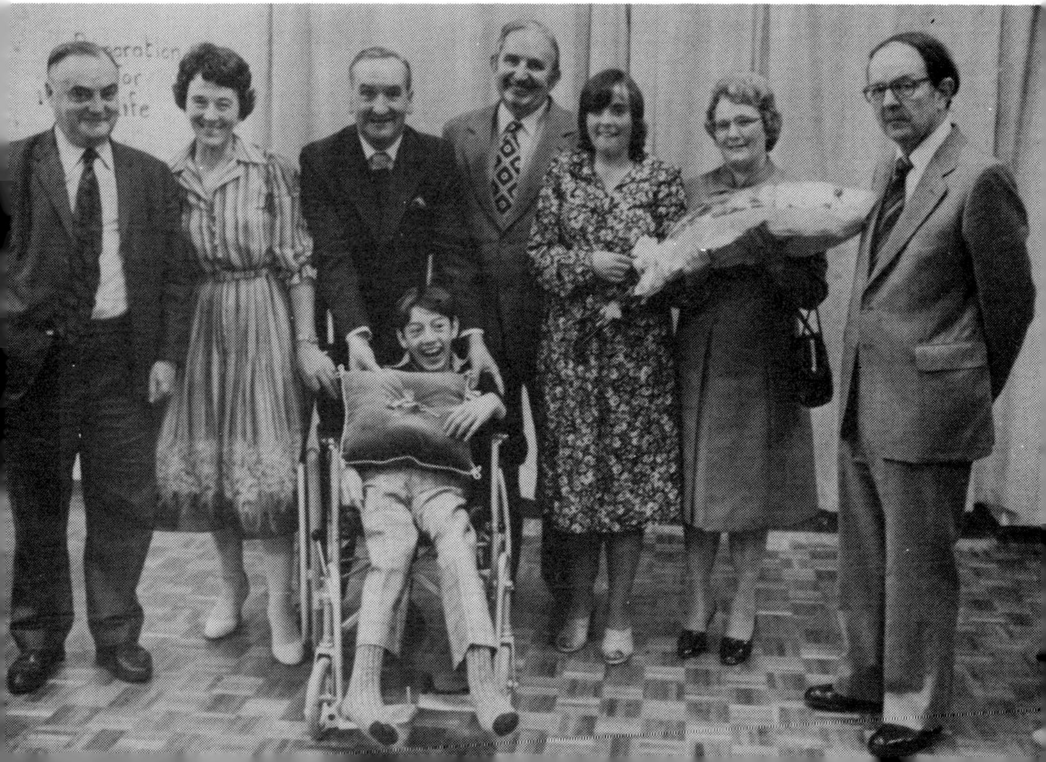

315—Dr. James Wakelin, Medical Practitioner since 1953 and Senior Partner of a Group Surgery Centre since 1955 to date

316—Members of the Pontypridd & Rhondda Hospital Management Committee 1974

317—East Glamorgan Hospital—a view known to patients and visitors

318—"Garth Olwg"—A home for the elderly, Church Village, opened by County Alderman Theophilus Griffiths on 17th August, 1966

DOCTOR PRICE, LLANTRISANT IN LLANTWIT FAERDREF

319—Penelopen and Nicholas Price, children of Dr. Wm. Price, Llantrisant, with a friend. Both children were baptised at St. Illtyd's Church in 1898

320—Miss Penelopen Price on 8th October, 1966, at Glyntaff Crematorium on the occasion of unveiling windows commemorating her father Dr. Wm. Price, Llantrisant. Our photograph shows Miss Price with members of the Burial Board, Alderman Theophilus Griffiths, Chairman Glamorgan C.C., Mr. Arthur Pearson, M.P., Mr. Jesse Warren and Chairman of the Pontypridd Urban D.C.

321—Dr. Wililam Price (1800-93) in Druid costume

THE FARMERS ARMS—HOSTELRY EXTRAORDINARY

322—The Farmers' Arms, Llanilltud Faerdref, in 1968. This hostelry has stood here since 1703 and in 1922 Mr. Jack Harries took over the licence. The family continued in business until Miss Minnie Harries, Miss Rachel Harries and Mrs. Sally Williams retired in June, 1977

1922 THE FARMERS' ARMS 1977

Thursday, 16th June, 1977

Up in the Old Church Village
  Amidst its lovely charms,
And near to the Old Church
  You'll find the Farmers' Arms,
This cosy little Tavern
  Stands dignified and bold,
And also as majestic
  As in the days of old.

Its patrons mostly local
  And some come from afar,
To spend a quiet evening
  Inside the cosy bar,
They have a chat together
  Of days that are gone by,
All with a pint before them
  A twinkle in their eye.

Within the Llantwit area
  Of all the Taverns there,
The Farmers' is the oldest
  Some old Folks still declare.
When you are in the district
  Admiring all its charms,
Before you leave, remember,
  Call at the Farmers' Arms.

Miss Minnie, and Miss Rachel,
  And Mrs. Williams too,
Will greet you when you enter,
  And take good care of you.
You will receive a welcome
  As given to a Star
By these three Lovely Ladies
  That serve behind the bar.

But now they have decided
  To leave the Farmers' Arms,
No more will they enchant us
  By their Sweet, Lovely Charms.
And soon they will be leaving
  Elsewhere their Home will be,
We wish them Health and Happiness
  Wherever they may be.

This family for eighty years
  Have served within this trade,
And far and wide, o'er many miles
  Sincere Friends they've made,
This evening some of those good friends
  Have gathered as you see,
To show appreciation to,
  This good, kind Family.

William John Lewis, J.P.
(Gwilym Llaeron)

323—A night to remember!—Thursday, 16th June, 1977, when regulars celebrated the retirement of Miss Minnie Harries, Licensee and her sisters. The presentation of gifts was made by Mr. Dillwyn Lewis, Beddau

324—Mr. Dillwyn Lewis, with Mrs. Sally Williams, Miss Minnie Harries and Miss Rachel Harries with their gifts. The evening marked an end of an era

325—Farmers' Arms—new hosts—Mrs. E. Venables and Mr. Terry Venables entertain Miss Rachel Harries and Mrs. Sally Williams, the former owners, on Friday, 2nd September, 1977—on the other side of the bar. Mr. Terry Venables is the Manager of Queens Park Rangers F.C. and writes the Hazel Detective Series on T.V.

PARISH CULTURE

326—Dressed in their Sunday best for a special occasion in the history of Carmel Chapel, Upper Boat in 1880's.

327—Tom Bryant, Royal Harpist (1882 - 1945) who lived in Carpenters' Arms, Efail Isaf

328—Miss Muriel E. Orsman, O.B.E., M.A., of Tyfica, Efail Isaf. Captain of W Ladies' Hockey Team 1923-30. Form Deputy Headmistress of Porth County Gr mar School for Girls; Glamorgan Cou Commissioner for Girl Guides; Co-author "The Land of the Red Dragon"; member many Welsh Youth Councils; member Representative and Governing Body of Church in Wales; member of Parochial Chu Council and Church Warden of the Parish Llantwit Fardre

329—Mr. Tom Powell, much respected and fondly remembered Librarian at Church Village, arriving in 1936 from the Rhondda. Always had an abiding interest in the history and well-being of the parish, a Deacon of Tabanacl Chapel, Efail Isaf. He died on 31st October, 1965

330—The Carnegie Library built in 1906 and administered by the Parish Council until 1965, when the County Council took over responsibility

331—The Cast "Princess Zara", an Operetta performed in Llantwit Fardre School, August, 1902

332 & 333—A favourite at the Town Hall Theatre, Pontypridd was Joy Clark and her Accordian Band, on stage here in 1943

334—Musical Comedies were regularly performed in the Mission Hall. Here is the Cast of "Magyar Melody" in 1947

335—The Dowlais Players present, "Olde Tyme Music Hall", as their first production at the new Community Centre in November, 1979. Their productions of plays and pantomimes continue to delight parishioners

336—Côr Godre'r Garth continues a long choral tradition in Efail Isaf. Here they are with a first Eisteddfod success and have received awards ever since

337—The Apollo Musical Arts Society distinguished themselves at the Waterford International Festival of Light Opera in September, 1980. Our photograph show Susan Jordan, awarded a principal prize of best comedienne and Dennis Williams was awarded the best individual from Wales. Their production was "My Fair Lady".

338—Civic Reception for award winners of "My Fair Lady", held at the Parish Hall, Church Village. The Community Council presented a cup to the Apollo Musical Arts Society to be awarded annually to members. The first award was made to Mrs. Elvira Davies during November, 1980, who has served the parish for over 60 years in musical circles

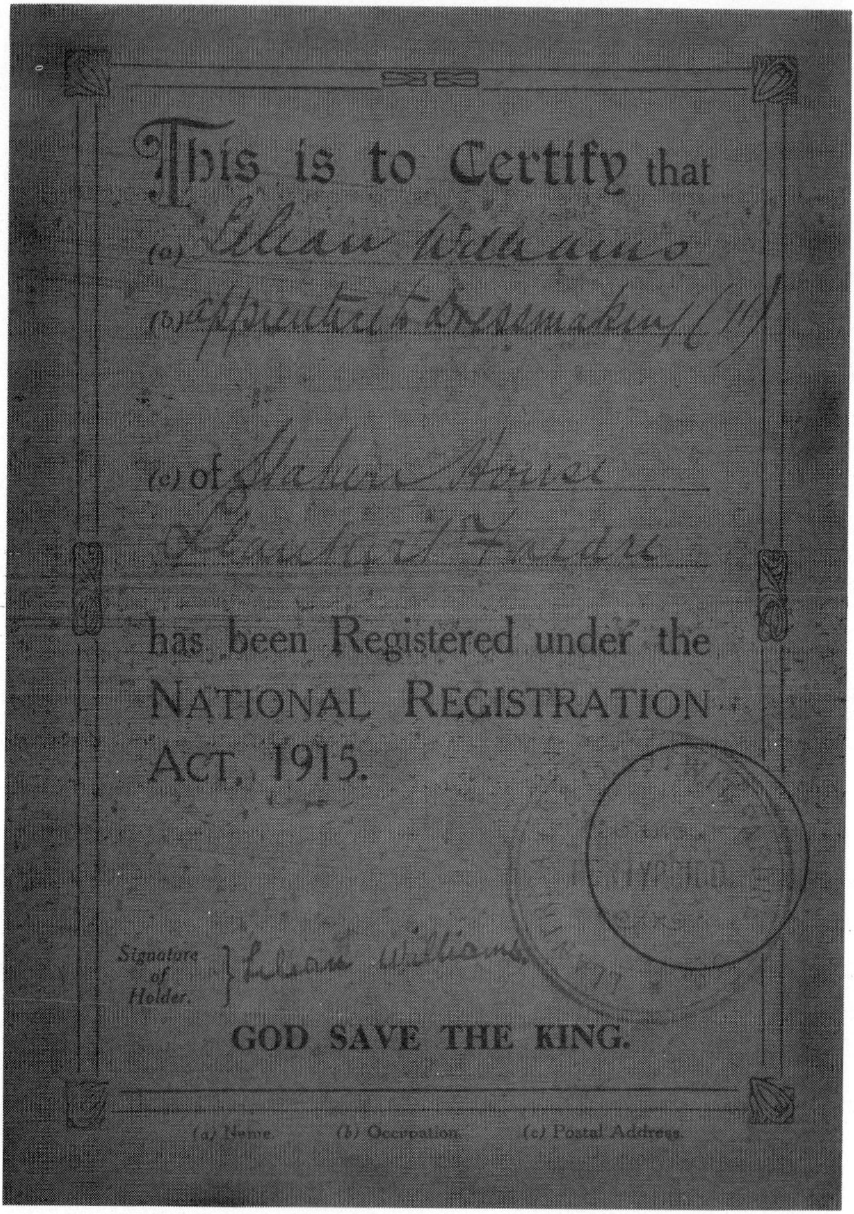

This is to Certify that

(a) Lilian Williams

(b)

(c) of

has been Registered under the NATIONAL REGISTRATION ACT, 1915.

Signature of Holder. } Lilian Williams

GOD SAVE THE KING.

(a) Name. (b) Occupation. (c) Postal Address.

339—Young Lillian Williams registers during World War I

340—Lillian Williams (left) in 1909 at School in Church Village

341—Tea at The Gables in 1916. Llantwit Faerdref Red Cross Detachment with Servicemen

342 & 343—Pontyclun Institute & Hospital during World War I, where members of the Llantwit Faerdref Red Cross attended on Servicemen—1916

344—Royal British Legion Officers of Llantwit Faerdref Branch in 1930

345—Presentation at the Crown Inn, Llantwit, 1934. H. K. Wiggins, Esq., President presenting Wm. Evans, Esq. with a Westminster Chimes Clock for valuable services rendered to the Beddau & District Branch of the British Legion, 8th February, 1934

346—Ladies' Group—knitting for the Troops, pictured here in 1940. They provided many garments for the Comforts' Fund

347—Air Raid Precautions and Civil Defence was all important. Here we see parishioners as Wardens, Ambulance Drivers—all prepared

348—Civil Defence Group of Wardens, Ambulance Drivers and the all important Messengers. All served 1939-1945

349—Members of the Special Constabulary formed during World War II. Pictured here at old Crown Hill Electric Works. This is the Llantwit Fardre Section in May, 1942

350—Air Raid Wardens pose for the camera at Garth Olwg before disbandment in 1945, after rendering important service to the community 1939-1945

351—The arrival of the Photographer was a special occasion. Here we see all the inhabitants of Efail Isaf on a day in 1884

352—A truly rural group pictured in 1919, near the Ceaser's Arms is Mr. William Collins, Licensee and friends

353—The Ceaser's Arms, Creigiau

354—The Carpenters' Arms, Efail Isaf

355—The Ship Inn, **Duffryn** Dowlais, Llantwit

356—The Three Horseshoes, Tonteg

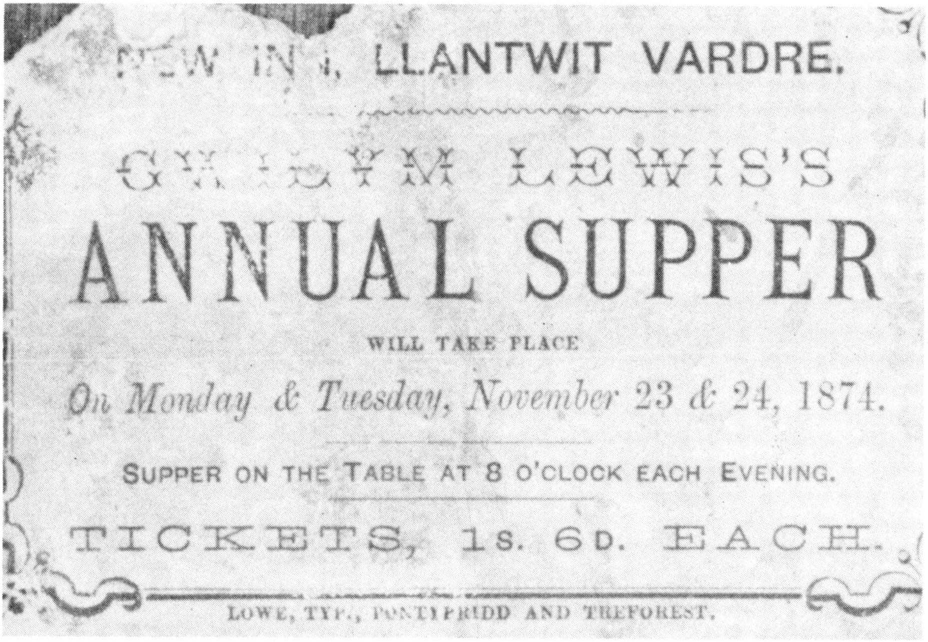

NEW INN, LLANTWIT VARDRE.

GWILYM LEWIS'S

ANNUAL SUPPER

WILL TAKE PLACE

On Monday & Tuesday, November 23 & 24, 1874.

SUPPER ON THE TABLE AT 8 O'CLOCK EACH EVENING.

TICKETS, 1s. 6d. EACH.

LOWE, TYP., PONTYPRIDD AND TREFOREST.

357—A souvenir of a pleasant evening at the New Inn

358—The first Scout Troop in Llantwit Faerdref. Photographed at Pontypridd in 1911

359—Church Village Constitutional Club "Tug of War Team", July, 1923. This building is now Bethel English Baptist Chapel

360—Bethel Baptist Chapel, Church Village

361—Opposite the Cross Inn stood the Cobbler's Shop. Our photograph shows Sam, the Cobbler with a happy apprentice, Martin Gay in 1920. The houses known as Percy Thomas' Row were demolished in 1950's and the site has new shops and a car park

362—Members of Church Village Youth Centre who were cup winners in County Drama Festival in 1950

363—The W.I. Scrapbook Committee meeting in the Library. The Scrapbook marked the Jubilee Year in 1966 of the W.I.

THE WOODLANDS

364—At Sunnyside, "Woodlands", members of the Royal British Legion in 1926

365—Dr. Washington Evans and a special day with the Royal British Legion in 1930

366—Mr. Gooch and family at the old stables, Woodlands, 1928

367—Woodlands Social Club Skittles Team, 1930

368—Woodlands Social Club Members, 1930

369—Dr. Washington Evans and Officials of Constitutional Club and District Council on the opening of the new Concert Hall in 1953

370—A group of workmen at the Cwm Colliery in the Twenties

371—The Twenties was a time of day trips in charabancs. Here we see members of the Cwm Colliery Ambulance Section setting out in 1920

372—A rare photograph recording the Church Village A.T.C. (Air Training Corps.) which trained teenagers during World War II. A very active group in the parish directed by Mr. George Mort

373—Rejoicing in the Parish Hall on V.J. Day—the end of World War II on 15th August, 1945

374—A rare photograph of members of the Cwm Colliery Band in 1926

375—Lady Luck comes to Llantwit Faerdref in 1934, when the syndicate pictured here won on an Irish Sweepstake ticket

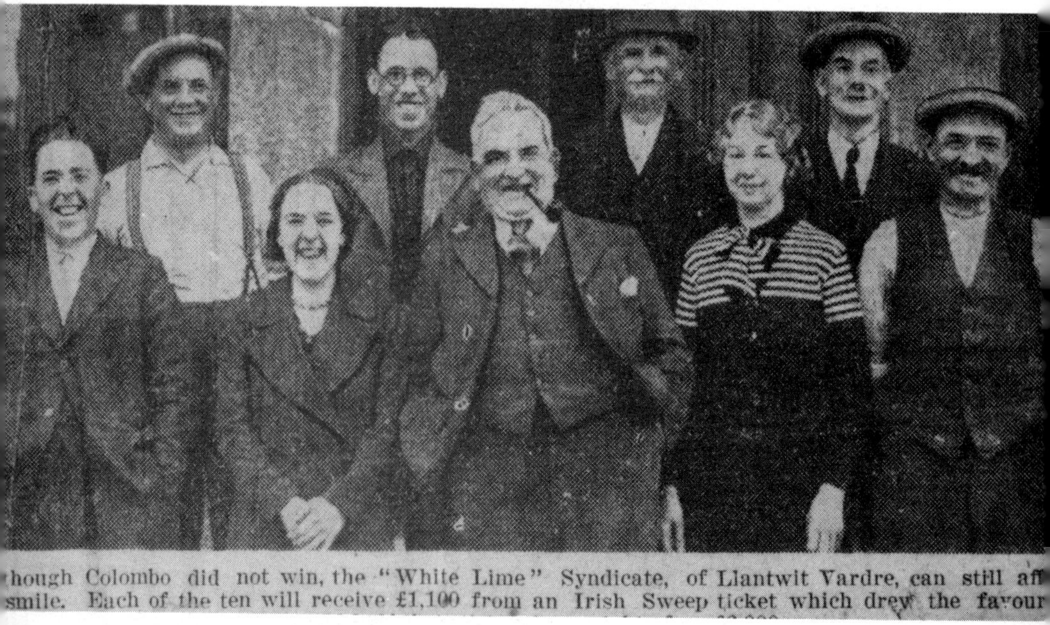

376—Chapel Outing to Porthcawl during the 1930's from Llantwit Faerdref

377—The Royal British Legion members with their children on an outing to Porthcawl in 1936

378—Parishioners on an outing to Blackpool in 1946

379—Members of the Royal Antediluvian Order of Buffaloes 1922

380—Presentation to Mr. Harry Palmer by members of the Royal Antediluvian Order of Buffaloes at the New Inn, Llantwit—Harry Palmer Lodge

381—A Civic Service at St. Illtyd's Church in 1956. District Councillor William John Lewis, J.P., Chairman, Llantrisant & Llantwit Faerdref R.D.C. with members of the Harry Palmer Lodge of Royal Antediluvian Order of Buffaloes

382—Mr. Barrie Collins, Mr. Brynmor John, M.P. at the Crown Inn for a Charity Walk Donation 1975. Harry Palmer Lodge (R.A.O.B.)

383—Festival Year 1951. Here we see parishioners gathered to plant trees in front of the Library on 10th November, 1951

384—Once again parishioners gather in celebration—A Christmas Party 1951

385—Members of the Women's Institute celebrate their Jubliee Year 1966, by presenting a seat at the entrance to Garth Olwg. Our photograph shows notable parishioners with Mr. Ken Pontin, Chairman of the Llantrisant & Llantwit Faerdref R.D.C.

386—Mr. William Young, renown as a Press Correspondent for the Local Press is here being presented, at the Crown Inn for Services to the Community

387—Jubilee Year 1935, and here we have the Parish Committee posing for the camera

388—Members of the Parish & Rural District Council at the Central Park, Church Village in 1939

389—The Village Hall Committee of 1952

390—Celebration of re-opening of the Mission Hall, after being redecorated, on 8th September, 1956

391—Members of the Crown Club on an outing to Rhayader Waterworks 1962

392—Coronation Year 1953. Llantwit celebrates with a party. Here we see Mrs. S. A. Bebb cutting the Coronation Cake with Rev. D. J. Howells and Mrs. Howells on 2nd June ,1953

393—Party time at the Mission Hall—Coronation of Queen Elizabeth II on 2nd June 1953

394—A rare photograph of Jubilee Celebrations on 6th May, 1935, at Llantwit Faerdref School where a party was enjoyed after a sports and carnival had been held for the enjoyment of all parishioners

395—Jubilee Year 1977. Children at Crown Hill celebrate the Jubilee of Queen Elizabeth II, 2nd June, 1977

396—Celebrating the Centenary of Beddau Board School on Tuesday, 29th September, 1977 are members of the Pontyclun Teachers' Association, by presenting Miss Clara Davies (centre, seated) at Tonteg Hospital, with gifts of fruit and flowers. Miss Davies, 95 years of age, was a pupil of the school and taught generations of pupils until her retirement in 1947. Miss Clara Davies was a first cousin to Ivor Novello, the actor/composer. She died 22nd December, 1977

397—This novel cake in the model of Beddau Board School was made by pupils at Bryn Celynnog Comprehensive School and presented to Miss Clara Davies during the Centenary Celebrations in September, 1977

398—A grand old lady who is the oldest person in Great Britain. Born at Llantrisant but in business at Commercial Street, Tynant. Miss Jeanette Thomas has served many parishioners at her haberdashery shop. Miss Thomas was 111 years old on Tuesday, 2nd December, 1980

399—A feature of modern life is the Day Centre for elderly persons. Here we see the Tŷ Illtyd Centre opened on Friday, 30th March, 1979. In the picture is Mr. Brynmor John, M.P. and Mr. Gwyn Breeze, Chairman, with members of the Community Council for Llantwit Faerdref

400—Establishing a new community takes time. Here we see Mr. Brian Rogers and Mr. John Williams, Chairmen of Project '77, unveiling a plaque at the opening of a new Community Hall at Crown Hill, Neuedd, Dowlais—opened Friday, 27th April, 1979

ROYAL VISIT TO LLANTWIT FARDRE ON THURSDAY, 6th NOVEMBER, 1980 BY H.R.H. PRINCESS ANNE

401—Royal visit to Crown Hill on Thursday, 6th November, 1980, by Her Royal Highness Princess Anne. Here she is arriving at the Community Hall, Llantwit

402—Official opening of the Scout & Guide Headquarters at Crown Hill, Llantwit by H.R.H. Princess Anne on Thursday, 6th November, 1980

403—First presentation of the Ann Lewis Award on Wednesday, 15th March, 1978 at Bryn Celynnog Comprehensive School. The Headmaster, Mr. J. G. Lloyd, B.Sc., looks on while Mr. Dillwyn Lewis makes the presentation to Mr. Jonathan Wilson, Tonteg. The award is presented annually and was established with royalties from the book, History of Llantrisant, by Dillwyn Lewis

404—Christmas 1979 brings Mr. Colin Davies, Head Porter at East Glamorgan Hospital, Church Village, international appreciation with 950 cards. Patients and visitors will know how valuable Mr. Davies' help and assurance is when attending the hospital—We all thank you!

405—A visit by the Bishop of Llandaff, Rev. John Poole-Hughes for the Civic Service of Community Councillor Luther Lodwig on Sunday, 23rd September, 1979 at St. Illtyd's Church. Our photograph shows Mr. & Mrs. Lodwig, Mr. Brynmor John, M.P., Mr. Alec Jones, M.P., Mayor and Mayoress of Taff Ely and Mr. Haydn Jones, Clerk to Community Council

406—Afternoon tea at the Vicarage when senior members of the Mothers' Union were entertained by Mrs. Shiela Williams, the Vicar, Rev. Arthur Williams and Curate, Rev. Alan Kettle in 1980

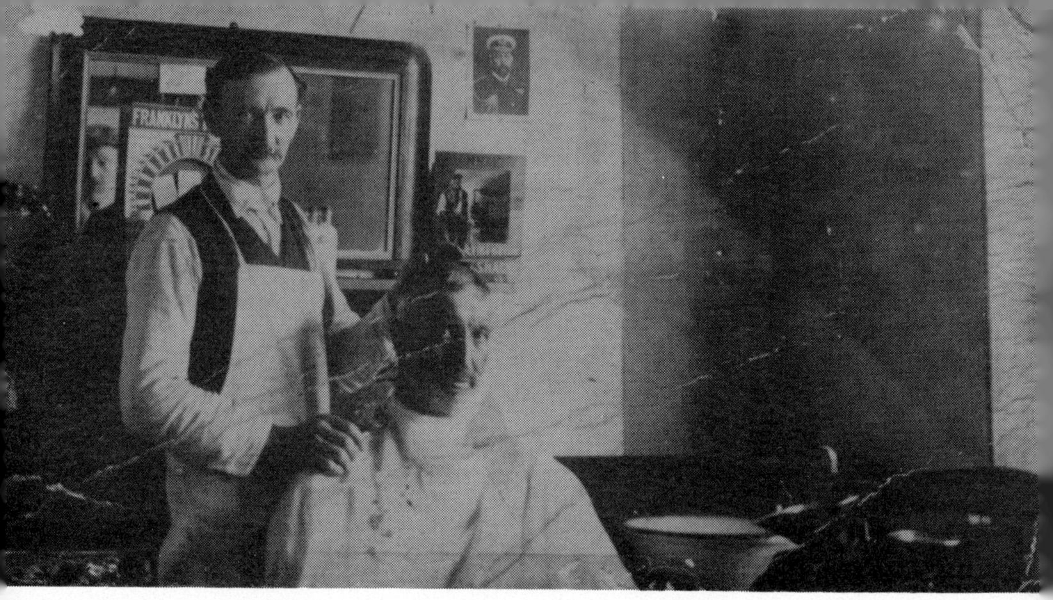

407—Hair Stylist at Tynant. Mr. Taylor's Salon 1916-26. Later a Mr. Thomas opened a Salon in Parish Road during 1930's and 1940's

THE LITTLE BARBER SHOP

Now there are many Barber Shops
  As you are well aware,
Where you can go and have a shave
  Or shorten your hair.
But there is one that beats the lot
  To go there is a treat,
And that's the Little Barber Shop
  That's in Commercial Street.

On entering by the sliding door
  Your eyes will open wide,
On seeing all those photographs
  Adorning the inside,
Thank God for those who have a flair
  For hobbies of this kind,
So that events of bygone days
  Can be brought back to mind.

The Barber is a jovial chap
  His partner sweet and gay
And when you're in the Barber's chair
  Your cares all fly away.
When next you want a little trim
  To make yourself look neat,
Call at the Little Barber Shop,
  That's in Commercial Street.

William John Lewis, J.P.
(Gwilym Llaeron)

408—Mr. Barrie Collins, Snr. a well-known Hairdresser since 1927

409—Mr. John Collins took over the family business in 1948. Mr. Barrie Collins supervised the newsagent end of the business while Mr. John Collins developed the hairdressing side. After 32 years of serving the community Messrs. B. & J. Collins has been transferred to Mr. Roy Ellis, who is to continue the business. An attraction has been the large and ever-changing display of local photographs. The shop became an interesting social centre. Our photograph shows Mr. John Collins and display of photographs. Mr. Collins retired, August, 1980, after 32 years in business

410—Mr. William (Chicken) Powell well-known interesting personality in the parish

411—Mr. John Jones known as 'Jone the Brickee', was a native of Towyn, Gwynedd and was the Clerk of Works/Foreman during the building of Council Houses at Beddau and Tonteg during the Twenties, retired 1946

SPORT

412—Llantwit United F.C. Team photograph taken 14th November, 1908

413—Llantwit Faerdref A.F.C. 1913-14 Season

414—Llantwit Faerdref R.F.C. 1919-20 Season. Outside the Queen's Hotel (The Coachhouse)

415—Upper Boat A.F.C. outside the Fox & Hounds 1916-17 Season

416—Llantwit Faerdref A.F.C. outside the Queen's Hotel in 1928

417—Cwm Colliery A.F.C. Cup Winners 1945

418—Hollybush Rangers A.F.C. 1921-22 Season

419—Church Village Junior A.F.C. 1922-23 Season

LLANILLTUD FAERDREF RUGBY FOOTBALL CLUB
Established 1946

420—Llanilltud Faerdref Rugby Football Club, President Dewi Chubb with Officers and Committee 1949-50

421—Llanilltud Faerdref R.F.C. Team 1949-50 Season when the Club was admitted to Welsh Rugby Union

422—Llanilltud Faerdref R.F.C. Team with their President Dewi Chubb during the 1952-53 Season

423—Llanilltud Faerdref R.F.C. Team on the Easter 1955 Tour

LLANILLTUD FAERDREF CRICKET CLUB

424—The original Llantwit Faerdref Cricket Team 1908

425—Llanilltud Faerdref Cricket Club 1956 wtih their President Mr. R. Hodgkinson, M.D., F.R.C.S., F.R.C.O.G.

426—Llantwit Faerdref Cricket Club 1957

427—Members of Llanilltud Faerdref Cricket Club in Porth, presentation of trophies for 1976

428--Llantwit Faerdref Cricket Club 1976 at the Connaught Rooms, Cardiff. Presentation by Sandy Aitken of Welsh Breweries of a trophy for winning the Glamorgan Alliance Cricket League

429—A red letter day at Llantwit in 1924 when Lady Megan Lloyd George visited and opened a fête

430—Mr. Aneurin Bunt—"The Singing, Whistling Shepherd", a Champion Shepherd and featured in B.B.C. film, "One Man and His Dog"

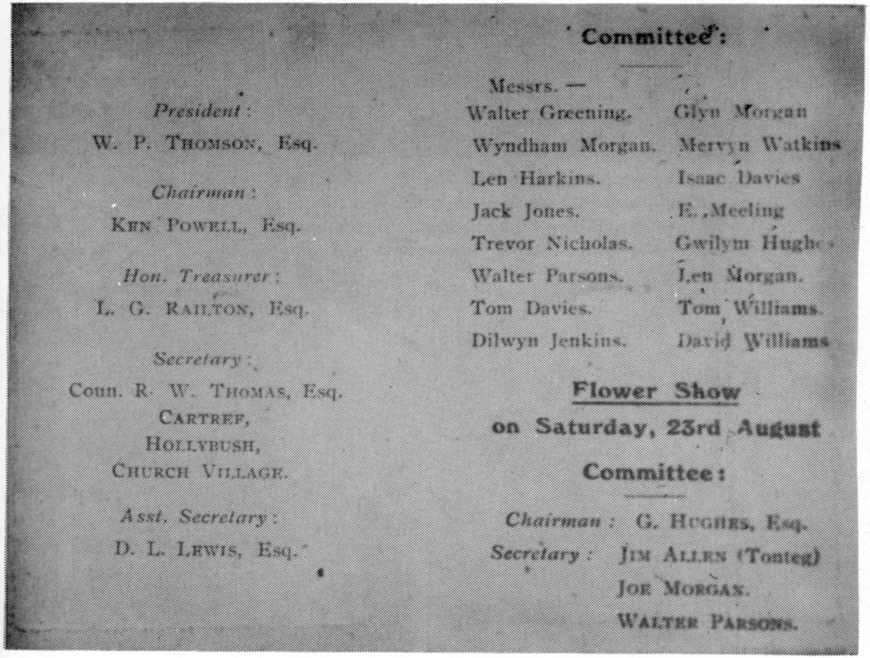

431 & 432—The original programme card cover and inside pages which give names of the original organisers

OFFICIALS AND LOCAL DIGNATORIES at the show. From left to right they are Mr. L. Lawrey, Mr. Ieuan Hughes, Mr. C. B. Banham, Mr. N. Taylor, Coun. L. Carter, Chairman of Llantrisant and Llantwit Fardre R.D.C.: Mr. Ian Kelsall, Secretary of Welsh C.B.I.: Mr. Bob Thomas, President; Mr. H. Taylor, Vice-Chairman; Mr. L. Bolderson, Chairman; Coun. L. T. Thomas, Chairman of the Parish Council; and Coun. C. Lewis, Cowbridge R.D.C.

433—Officials and Guests at the 1973 Show

434 & 435—The 1973 Show. The Llantwit Fardre & District Horse & Agricultural Show is an established annual event and continues to raise funds for several charities

436—A Prize Bull outside the Butcher's Shop of Mr. Arthur Smith, Church Village, with Parish Councillor Cubert Matthews

438—Mr. Oliver Thomas, noted Soccer Referee from Llantwit

437—H. Hopkins, who played for Crystal Palace F.C. in 1926

439—Mr. Fred Alford, Champion Cyclist 1936

440—Mr. Jefferey Lloyd of Tonteg, the first Welshman to swim the English Channel 1978. Here we see him coming ashore at Porthcawl after a record-breaking swim of the Bristol Channel in 1979. Mr. Lloyd was given a Civic Reception on 14th January, 1979 by Llantwit Faerdref Community Council

Back on land, Jeff Lloyd at Porthcawl after his latest swimming achieve

441—The British Ambassador to Belgium presenting the B.E.M. to Graham Romford Thomas in 1974 for services to the Royal Air Force. Graham Thomas was a founder member of the Red Arrows Team 1968-72

442—Penycoedcae Church b. 1875

443—Major Richard Hale-Mole 1890.
Penycoedcae House

444—Ty'n y Nant Farm, home of Williams' Family for over 500 years until 1966. The building was demolished in 1969

445—Mr. & Mrs. Ebenezer Williams, Son and Dog, Ty'n y Nant Farm. Mr. Williams was the Rate Collector for the parish

446—Tir Mab Ellis House, the Hewett Family home

447—John Hewett, J.P., D.L. (1786-1868), Honorary Colonel Glamorganshire Artillery Volunteers

448—The Creigiau Pottery founded by Mr. Southcliffe in 1947

TRADITIONS

As represented by pupils of Maesybryn Primary School. December 1980 in "Compliments of the Seasons"

449—'Marie Lwyd' ancient Welsh ceremony enacted on New Year's Eve

450—Christmas Nativity Scene

451—An Old Mummers' Play

452—Punch and Judy